ALABASTER TOMBS

1. Northleigh (Oxon), Wilcote Chapel

ALABASTER TOMBS

of the

PRE-REFORMATION PERIOD
IN ENGLAND

by

ARTHUR GARDNER
M.A., F.S.A.

CAMBRIDGE
at the
UNIVERSITY PRESS
1940

CAMBRIDGE UNIVERSITY PRESS
Cambridge, New York, Melbourne, Madrid, Cape Town, Singapore,
São Paulo, Delhi, Dubai, Tokyo, Mexico City

Cambridge University Press
The Edinburgh Building, Cambridge CB2 8RU, UK

Published in the United States of America by Cambridge University Press, New York

www.cambridge.org
Information on this title: www.cambridge.org/9780521166201

© Cambridge University Press 1940

First published 1940
First paperback edition 2010

A catalogue record for this publication is available from the British Library

ISBN 978-0-521-16620-1 Paperback

CONTENTS

LIST OF ILLUSTRATIONS

INTRODUCTION

A number of books have been published dealing with the tombs and monumental effigies of medieval England, but the older antiquaries were more interested in the genealogical side of the subject, and in the identification of the persons to whom the monuments were erected, than in the style of the sculpture and classification of them. For the latter purpose only the most accurate of drawings can compete with modern photography, and then only in cases when a measured drawing can be made from a position to which it is difficult to hoist a camera. Very valuable work was produced by such writers as Weaver, Blore, Gough, Richardson, Hollis and Stothard, and the splendid tome on the *Monumental Effigies of Great Britain* published by the last-named in 1817 is a remarkable record of research and accurate draughtsmanship. In most of these works comparatively little attention was paid to the materials used, while the late Prof. Edward S. Prior, with whom the present author had the privilege of collaborating in *Medieval Figure Sculpture in England*, has pointed out that this question of the materials used is one of the chief keys to any study of sculptural style. Among modern books Mr F. H. Crossley's magnificently illustrated volume *English Church Monuments* deals with all classes of tombs down to the end of the medieval period, but leaves room for a more detailed treatment of the last phase of the subject during which the productions of the alabaster workmen were the most characteristic examples.

Ever since Sir William St John Hope's valuable paper 'On the early working of alabaster in England' was published in the *Archaeological Journal* for 1904, a considerable amount of attention has been given to the English school of alabaster workers which flourished during the fourteenth, fifteenth and sixteenth centuries. Notice, however, has been mainly directed to the retables which have mostly been broken up and scattered and so afford opportunities to collectors which the tombs can never give. Several interesting papers have been published in the *Archaeological Journal* by Dr Philip Nelson, F.S.A., Dr W. L. Hildburgh, F.S.A. and others on these 'tables' as they are called, but the still more important examples of the productions of the alabaster men, the tombs, had only been treated in sections or chapters in larger and more comprehensive works until the publication of an article by the present writer in the *Archaeological Journal* for 1923. This volume is a revision and expansion of that article, and contains most of the illustrations prepared for that paper together with others from *Medieval Sculpture in England* and Prior and Gardner's *Medieval Figure Sculpture* and a number of fresh blocks specially made to fill up the gaps and give a more complete picture of the subject under review. In it an attempt is made to list and classify the surviving alabaster monuments from the earliest examples *c.* 1330 down to the time of the Reformation, which for this purpose may be placed *c.* 1530–40, and to describe the changes in treatment, in costume and armour during that period. It does not attempt any serious research into genealogical problems, which requires separate treatment by a specialist in that department, though a survey of the material available, and a system for dating the monuments, may afford a basis on which those interested in such subjects may build.

The compilation of the lists at the end of the book have necessitated a great deal of travel and research, as the ground has never been fully explored for such a purpose. It will be many years before the Royal Commission on Ancient Monuments can extend its researches over the whole country on

the plan so admirably initiated in Hertfordshire, Buckingham-
shire, Essex, Herefordshire, Westminster and Wales, and the
various local guide-books vary so much in quality and re-
liability that a complete survey is very difficult. The *Little
Guides* to the counties have given valuable assistance, but
these vary according to the special interests of the authors,
and it is only in some of them that attention is paid to the
material of tombs described. In certain counties the local
antiquarian societies have published lists of their own monuments, of which the following have been most helpful: Dr A. C.
Fryer, F.S.A. has published a series of illustrated articles on
'Monumental Effigies in Somerset' in the *Proceedings of the
Somersetshire Archaeological and Natural History Society*, and
Mr Philip B. Chatwin, F.R.I.B.A. has published a most
valuable article on 'Monumental Effigies in Warwickshire'
in the *Transactions of the Birmingham Archaeological Society*, vols.
XLVII and XLVIII, 1921 and 1922, with careful descriptions
and full illustration. Mr F. H. Crossley, F.S.A., whose superb
photographs of this kind of subject are well known, has
published a full account of the effigies of Cheshire in the
Transactions of the Historical Society of Lancashire and Cheshire,
1925. Messrs H. Lawrance and T. E. Routh have under-
taken a series of articles in the *Derbyshire Arch. and Nat. Hist.
Society's Journal*, 1925, dealing with the 'Military Effigies of
Derbyshire'. Mr C. H. Hunter Blair has published the
Medieval Effigies in County Durham and those in North-
umberland in *Archaeologia Aeliana*, vol. VI, 1929, and vol. VII,
1930, and Canon Bower has listed those of the diocese of
Carlisle in the *Transactions of the Cumberland and Westmorland
Antiquarian Society*, vol. XV, 1899, though he occasionally
omits to state the material. A. Hartshorne described the
Recumbent Monumental Effigies of Northamptonshire as long ago
as 1876.

Arms, Armour and Alabaster round Nottingham, by the late

G. Fellows, describes and illustrates in detail a number of monuments in that neighbourhood.

The first article dealing with our subject was probably that contributed to the *Archaeological Journal* by E. Richardson as long ago as 1853. Sir William St John Hope's paper, referred to above, published in· 1904, expanded and brought up to date Richardson's notes, drew attention to the varied activities of the alabaster men in reredoses as well as tombs, and proved that many of such objects distributed in churches and tombs all over Europe, and as far away as Iceland, were products not of Flemish workshops, as had often been suggested, but of those of Nottingham and other centres in England.

In compiling the lists at the end of the book I have to acknowledge generous help from a number of friends in addition to the published information referred to above. The late Mr F. E. Howard, whose premature death was a great loss to English Archaeology, allowed me to check my lists with one which he had begun to compile for his own use, and helped me to fill up several gaps from it. The late Mr W. M. I'Anson generously placed his unrivalled knowledge of the Yorkshire effigies at my disposal, and Mr P. B. Chatwin, whose valuable paper on the Warwickshire effigies has already been mentioned, has helped also with Worcestershire and Staffordshire. Messrs T. E. Routh and F. H. Crossley, the Rev. T. Romans, the late Dr A. C. Fryer and Dr Philip Nelson have given me valuable local information, and a number of other friends have supplied useful details and hints. Mr J. G. Mann, Keeper of the Wallace Collection and of the Tower Armoury, has given me valuable advice about questions of armour, and his paper on the post-Reformation tombs, published by the Walpole Society, carries on the story for the period immediately following that treated in this book. Due acknowledgment should also be made to

Messrs Kelly and Schwabe's excellent *Short History of Costume and Armour*, which gives the latest and most up-to-date information on the subject.

Finally I have to thank the clergy, vergers and other guardians of the monuments throughout the country for permits and facilities readily granted for studying and photographing them.

A. G.

November 1939

CHAPTER I

THE ALABASTER MEN

The lists at the end of this volume include some 342 tombs, with 507 alabaster effigies,[1] counting husband and wife separately when they occur on the same tomb. There are, no doubt, a few others scattered about the country which have escaped my notice, but it would be reasonable to guess that the total of those still existing does not much exceed 520 examples altogether. The above figures refer to tombs of the Gothic period down to about 1540, though a few may have been included in our period VI which retain a Gothic character, even if mixed to some extent with Renaissance details. The number might be increased by including others *c.* 1530–60, which retain some Gothic feeling, as it is difficult to draw a hard and fast line at any particular date. Such a tomb, for instance, as that of the Earl of Huntingdon (d. 1561) at Ashby-de-la-Zouch (302), exhibits much more Gothic than Italian feeling in its whole design and treatment, apart from a few insignificant details.

The use of alabaster for tombs continued right through the sixteenth century, though often mixed with varied marbles, and many tombs of the Elizabethan period attain high artistic value, though they cannot be dealt with here.

Alabaster tombs are naturally most numerous in the counties of Derby and Nottingham in the immediate neighbourhood of the medieval quarries at Tutbury and Chellaston, but they are plentiful throughout Yorkshire and the Midlands, and there is hardly a county that cannot boast a number of

---

[1] The present writer has himself examined and photographed practically all of these, and can therefore guarantee the accuracy of most of the details recorded.

examples. The largest collections of alabaster effigies are at
Harewood, 12; Macclesfield, 7; Westminster, Canterbury,
Ashbourne, Bromsgrove, Llandaff and Tong, 6 each. Just as
in the thirteenth century the Purbeck marblers set the fashion
for all the tomb-makers, so in the fifteenth the alabaster
workshops produced the monuments for all the most important people, and set up a standard copied at more or less
distance by the humbler workers in freestone.

The English alabaster, or gypsum, is a peculiar form of
sulphate of lime, and is a material quite different from the
oriental or continental alabaster. Most of the earlier tombs
are made of a pure white variety, but towards the end of our
period the finer beds seem to have begun to give out and
brown-veined and streaky blocks came into use. Where
monuments have been restored it is sometimes a help in
recognising the new portions to find that the repairs have been
executed in the streaky material. Alabaster is soft and easy
to work, well suited for fine detail, and takes colour and
gilding splendidly. When not exposed to the weather it retains
its original surface, and we are better able to realise the
gorgeous effect of these medieval monuments than in the case
of the earlier freestone figures, depending for their full effect
on gesso and paint, to which time has been less kind. The
softness of the alabaster, however, has rendered it peculiarly
liable to damage at the hands of the initial-cutting fiends of
the last century,[1] and many a priceless work of art has been

---

[1] The chapel containing the fine collection of effigies at Abergavenny
was for many years used as a school, which naturally resulted in serious
damage to the figures. But the abominable habit of initial-cutting was
not confined to the eighteenth or nineteenth centuries; in one place I was
pointed out the initials of J. B., which were said to be those of John
Bradshaw, Cromwell's lieutenant. An even earlier example is given by
Prof. Lethaby in his *Westminster Abbey re-examined*, p. 276, where he claims
to have discovered the name YPESWIC scratched under the canopy on
Crouchback's tomb, which he identifies as that of a sacrist in the later
fourteenth century named Ipswich.

hopelessly ruined by the activity of these vandals. Even to-day, though better care is usually taken of our ancient churches, it is a pity that our schools do not do more to cultivate the aesthetic faculties of our young barbarians, and to encourage reverence for things of beauty or historic interest.

The first known use of alabaster for carved work occurs in one of the inner orders of the rich Norman west doorway of Tutbury Priory church, in the immediate neighbourhood of the quarries (2). Now Tutbury was given by Henry III to his son Edmund, Earl of Lancaster, passed to his successors the earls and dukes, and remains to-day a portion of the duchy. It is possible that this royal connexion of the place may have had something to do with the royal patronage of the alabaster workers when their productions first came into prominence, as will be described when we come to deal with the effigies. John of Gaunt largely rebuilt Tutbury Castle, and his tomb in old St Paul's had alabaster effigies under a magnificent canopy.[1] It was set up during his lifetime on the death of his first wife.

In his interesting paper on 'Monumental Effigies in Warwickshire' (*Birm. Arch. Soc. Transactions*, vol. XLVII (1921)) Mr P. B. Chatwin quotes from *John of Gaunt's Register* for 1374 (no. 1394, 13 June) instructions given by that prince to his agent at Tutbury to send six cartloads of alabaster for the construction of a tomb for his wife Blanche, who had just died. Two special blocks were to be selected for the principal figures, and if not available at Tutbury they were to be sought elsewhere (probably at Chellaston). This suggests that the actual carving was done in London, and the materials imported for that purpose. London, of course, has no stone quarries near at hand, and Purbeck marble from Corfe or Caen stone from Normandy had been imported by sea for

---

[1] See Dugdale, *History of St Paul's*, p. 60, with illustration by Hollar.

the finer work, so that it would have been natural to send for the alabaster in block for the newest fashion of tomb.[1] The earliest group of alabaster tombs, which are usually of mixed materials, as far as tomb chest and canopy are concerned, may therefore be assigned with some probability to London workshops.

As the trade developed it would be natural to expect to find it centring round the neighbourhood of the quarries, and there is considerable evidence that this was actually what happened. St John Hope points out that in 1367 Peter the mason, of Nottingham, was paid for a great reredos to be erected at Windsor, which was so important a work that it required ten eight-horsed carts to transport it from Nottingham to Windsor.[2] For the following century Hope was able to publish a number of references to alabaster men, or 'alablaster men' as they were often called, working in Nottingham, and supplying the 'tables' or small reliefs of which the retables were composed. There are also records of them at York, Lincoln, Norwich and at the end of our period at Burton-on-Trent. In Tutbury Priory itself there was a tomb of alabaster erected for Henry de Ferrers by the Earl of Derby. It has thus become the rule in most museums to label these alabaster carvings as 'School of Nottingham'.

The survival of a very large proportion of alabaster tombs in the counties nearest the quarries also points to the presence of workshops either at the quarries themselves, or in Nottingham or adjacent towns. Possibly the larger blocks needed for the tombs were worked at Chellaston beside the best quarry there, while smaller blocks were taken to Nottingham to be worked up into the retables. We have, too, the well-known contract for the tomb of Ralph Greene, Esquire, who died in

---

[1] Purbeck marble was sometimes referred to as 'marmor regis', and may have been introduced at first under royal patronage in the same way.
[2] Pipe Roll, 41 Edward III, m. 41.

1418, which still remains in Lowick Church, Northampton-shire. The original, which was in medieval French, is lost, but was published in a rare work, *Halstead's Genealogies*, and reprinted by A. Hartshorne in his *Recumbent Effigies of North-amptonshire*. Long extracts in English have been published by Hope in the above-mentioned article, and by Mr Crossley in his *English Church Monuments*. It was drawn up between the executors and Katharine the widow and Thomas Prentys and Robert Sutton, of Chellaston, 'kervers', who undertook to set up the tomb before Easter 1420 for a sum of £40 sterling, the equivalent, of course, of a far higher sum to-day. The tomb was to be of the finest alabaster, and exact measure-ments were fixed. On it were to be placed two images, one the counterfeit of an esquire armed at all points, with a helm under his head and a bear at his feet; and the other the counterfeit of a lady lying in her open surcoat with two angels holding a pillow under her head, and two little dogs at her feet, the one of the said images holding the other by the hand. Two tabernacles called *gablettes* were to be at their heads, and the sides of the tomb were to have images of angels bearing shields according to the device of the widow and executors. The whole was to be decorated with painting and gilding, and an arch of alabaster with pendants and cresting was to be placed above the tomb. This arch no longer survives over the tomb at Lowick (5), which corresponds in all other respects, apart from the fading of the colours, with the specification. In no case has such a canopy of alabaster survived, though erections in stone, and in a few later in-stances of Purbeck marble,[1] may be found scattered about the country.

Several other important monuments of about the same

---

[1] E.g. at Melbury Sampford in Dorset. It is doubtful, however, if these were designed for their present purpose, as they look later than the effigies they contain.

date show such similar design that it has been suggested that they came from the same workshop. Very similar *gablettes* occur on the magnificent tombs of Thomas, Earl of Arundel (d. 1416) at Arundel (6) and of King Henry IV (d. 1413) at Canterbury (182, 185), and if we can attribute these to the Prentys and Sutton firm we must regard Chellaston as the leading monumental *atelier* of the day. The effigies on the tomb at Ashwellthorpe, Norfolk (84, 85), too, have so close a resemblance to those of Lowick that we may assign them to the same sculptors with some confidence.

Unfortunately we have no other definite record of the provenance of these monuments, though it is possible to group a certain number of them together as of similar origin. Thus the tombs at Swine (14) with their unusual kneeling angels and the later series at Harewood (17) and Methley (18) might, from their geographical position, be assigned to the alabaster men of York.

If the tomb at Sheriff-Hutton, Yorks (267), attributed to Edward, Prince of Wales, young son of Richard III, who died in 1484, belongs to the fragment of the tomb chest preserved in the church, the likeness of the design to the Methley tomb would suggest doubts as to the identification. It is difficult to speak with certainty as this tomb is so worn and mutilated as to make confident deductions from its style impossible, but it certainly has a look of the Harewood and Methley monuments of fifty years earlier, and the figure of the prince himself suggests the same heavy and rather coarse treatment of the Harewood knight.

The knights at Willoughby-in-the-Wolds (158) and Merevale (170) are so alike, not only in details of equipment, but in the treatment of them, that they have struck more than one observer as the work of the same hand.[1] The small rudi-

---

[1] See P. B. Chatwin in 'Monumental Effigies in Warwickshire', *Trans. Birm. Arch. Soc.* vol. XLVII (1921), p. 59.

mentary tassels suspended from the fauld and the peculiar bascinet with long back projection, which seems a forerunner of the salet, are exactly alike in both cases. Here, however, the tomb chests are evidently by different hands, which suggests that sometimes the effigies were ordered in one place and the rest of the tomb in another, or perhaps the tomb chests might have been made locally, and only the important figures ordered from the famous workshop at Chellaston, or Nottingham. The knight and lady at East Shefford, Berks (173), might perhaps be also attributed to this sculptor.

The simple tomb with angels at intervals, and two flying angels supporting a shield at the end, which occurs in Judge Gascoigne's monument at Harewood (15), is closely matched in the tomb of a civilian at Aston-on-Trent (151), to be described later. Another civilian at Harlaxton would seem to be by the same hand, and we therefore have another group of three remarkable tombs which seem to be of common origin.

Another group, which includes some of the finest of our alabaster knights of the second quarter of the fifteenth century, at Tong, Dennington, Over Peover, Bromsgrove, Porlock (181, 176, 199, 91, 172), Dunster, etc. might be regarded as coming from the successors of the Prentys and Sutton workshop at Chellaston.

At the same time London was, no doubt, producing monuments of the imported material. There are records of destroyed tombs in the church of the Grey Friars, the Charter-house and old St Paul's, which would naturally be the products of London workshops, and in 1376 there is a payment to John Orchard '*Latoner*' of London for making the bronze weepers for Queen Philippa's tomb, and also for the little alabaster tomb which still stands in the abbey to the infant children of Edward III (74). This suggests that John Orchard kept an establishment for providing monuments in varied materials, such as existed at the end of our period when we find a contractor like Drawswerd, M.P. and Mayor of York, sending in designs for Henry VII's tomb. There is, further, a record of a great reredos of alabaster for Durham Cathedral being packed in boxes in London in order to be sent to its destination by sea. It is, of course, possible that the alabaster figures and reliefs were sent to London from Nottingham to be incorporated in their stone or wood setting, but it seems more natural to regard this as a London work.

At the beginning of the sixteenth century some specially fine monuments stand by themselves in the treatment of figures and weepers; those at Windsor (279), Aldermaston (57), and Fawsley (274), for instance, form a group quite distinct in character from the tombs at Ratcliffe-on-Soar (247), Eye (Herefordshire) (255), etc., which may be taken as the typical products of the Chellaston-Nottingham school. At Fawsley (60), curiously enough, the weepers are set against a dark background, in the same way as in our earliest example, that of Prince John of Eltham at Westminster (12, 13), which we have taken as a London work. Little columns looking something like metal water-pipes are placed on each side of the niche containing the weepers, and may be a trick of a special workshop. As, however, these occur also in contemporary tombs at Abergavenny, Leigh (Staffordshire), Malpas, Tong (25) and Elford (26), it cannot be taken as a definite indication. Possibly it may point to Burton rather than London. All these attributions, however, must only be regarded as purely conjectural, as the Lowick contract is the only definite record which we have connecting an extant alabaster tomb with a particular workshop.

If a small detail may be allowed significance, there is a little pattern consisting of a four-leaved flower separated from the next by two cross cuts, shown in the Staindrop tomb (93), which is used to decorate narrow bands of ornament, especially those covering the long side joints of arm and leg armour. This occurs in many of the more ornate figures of the whole of the first half of the fifteenth century, in the later transitional effigies of our camail knights of class II, as well as in class III. It lasts too long and is too universal to have been the monopoly of a particular workshop, as it lasted for thirty or forty years, from the knight at Clifton, *c.* 1400 (140), to the Tideswell figure of *c.* 1430–40 (169). We might perhaps regard it as a stock pattern handed down through two or three generations in a big school such as that at Nottingham. Besides Clifton and Tideswell it may be found at Swine, Staindrop, Elford, Bottesford, Haversham, Weobley, East Shefford, etc.

Leland, writing in the time of Henry VIII, reported that 'at Burton are many marbellers working in alabaster', and Hope has found a record of one Robert Bocher 'alablastur-man' working there in 1481. Records of medieval tombs being made in that centre are scarce, though we have some from the reign of Elizabeth, by which time the pure white beds at Chellaston would seem to have become exhausted for large blocks, and the streaky varieties were being used, often in combination with varied-coloured marbles.

Mr P. B. Chatwin, F.S.A., whose valuable paper on the Warwickshire effigies has several times been quoted, draws attention to a contract of 1510,[1] whereby Henry Harpur and William Moorecock of Burton undertake to make a tomb for Henry Foljamb at Chesterfield, which still exists. This has no effigy, being surmounted by a brass, but the delicately wrought weepers are distinctive, and can be matched almost exactly by others at Cubley (8). In the contract it was specified that the Chesterfield tomb should be made as good as that at Cubley. We have, therefore, here something to go

---

[1] *Collectanea Topographica et Genealogica*, vol. I, p. 354, quoted by P. B. Chatwin in *Birm. Arch. Soc. Transactions*, 1923.

upon in assigning tombs to the Burton firm. The weepers
of the Babyngton monument at Ashover (61) must be by the
same hand, and as the effigies at Ashover and of the Blythe
tomb at Norton, near Sheffield, seem closely allied, we may
reasonably assign both these tombs to the Burton carvers.
The canopies of the tomb chest of the tomb of Sir William
Mathew at Llandaff are also almost replicas of those of this
group; and though the weepers have not quite the delicacy
of those at Ashover, and are mixed with standing friars, we
may allow this also to be a Burton work. Mr Chatwin goes
further and assigns a later group of monuments, *c.* 1530–40,
to the same source, or to an allied workshop. He is certainly
right in claiming a common origin for the tombs at Castle
Donington (262) and Clifton Campville (68), which are
almost duplicates. The weepers consist of angels of a heavy
type, and seated friars, or bedesmen, under wide round
arched niches on coarse semi-classical columns, with clumsy
shallow cusping round the arches. Very similar treatment is
found at Duffield (265), and later still at Ross (52). The two
tombs at Prestwold and another at North Aston (34) also
have the friar weepers though the arcading is of a slightly
different type. The likeness, however, is enough to justify
ascription to the same shop, and Mr Chatwin has some
justification in assigning them to Burton sculptors, though
probably they are not the work of the Harpur and Moorecock
firm, but of a younger establishment to some extent influenced
by their predecessors. The same writer points out that a
number of tomb chests of about the middle of the sixteenth
century have pilasters at the ends ornamented with vases;
these may be taken as a kind of signature of the Burton
school.

The elaborately niched monuments of Sir William Smythe
at Elford (26), and of Richard Vernon at Tong (25), must
have come from another workshop, and another hand again

may be recognised in the very similar figures at Batley (261), Thurlaston (260) and a tomb at Abergavenny.

Sir Henry Pierrepont at Holme Pierrepont, Sir John Strelley at Strelley and the Earl of Wiltshire at Lowick (209), all lie upon tombs, the sides of which are decorated with a simple cusped lozenge pattern, which becomes a stock pattern later, as in the tomb at Ratcliffe-on-Soar (77), but there is a family likeness in the earlier set of effigies which may justify us in grouping them together.

There is a remarkable likeness between the late fifteenth-century knights and ladies at Chilton, Suffolk, and Wethersfield, Essex (282, 283). In both cases the knights wear tabards and are of a heavily built type rather plainly wrought in a manner that differs from the northern examples. Their ladies are also very much alike, though one has the Lancastrian and the other the Yorkist collar, one of the rare instances where the wife has this decoration and the husband is without it. It looks as though the two families had ordered the tombs from the same sculptor in emulation of one another. In view of the geographical situation it would not be unreasonable to claim these as examples of London work at this period, but this is pure guesswork.

Interesting light is thrown on the reputation of the English alabaster workers by a royal passport[1] granted for the export of a tomb to Nantes in 1408 to be placed over the grave of John, Duke of Brittany, the former husband of Joan of Navarre, queen of Henry IV. This was made by Thomas Colyn, Thomas Holewell and Thomas Poppehowe, but nothing further is known about these men or where they worked. The monument was destroyed in the French Revolution, but a good drawing of it was published in Lobineau's *Histoire de Bretagne*, and has recently been reproduced by

---

[1] T. Rymer, *Foedera*, vol. VIII, p. 510.

Mr Crossley. The effigy must have been very like that of the Earl of Westmorland at Staindrop, except that a slender circlet endorsed the bascinet in place of the orle (see p. 40) of the Staindrop tomb, which must be dated some years later. The design of the tomb chest is of a similar type in both these monuments, the later one being slightly more elaborate.

In this connexion it is worth while to note a writ issued by the king in 1382 to allow the Pope's collector, Cosmato Gentilis, to take back with him to Rome three large images in alabaster of the Virgin, St Peter and St Paul, and a smaller one of the Holy Trinity. There is thus evidence that the English alabaster shops were exporting their wares long before the Reformation; we must therefore allow that the numerous examples of their work scattered over Europe were not all the spoils cast out of our churches by the Reformers.[1]

---

[1] Another instance of the export of the products of the English alabaster shops is given by Dr Hildburgh in the *Antiquaries Journal* for July 1926. A reredos was presented to the Cathedral of Santiago de Compostela by an English priest, and is still preserved there. As it illustrates the legend of St James it must have been specially ordered for the purpose.

Dr Philip Nelson, in the *Archaeological Journal* 1920, quotes an application from Henry and William Mayn, merchants of Dartmouth, in 1390, for permission to export alabaster images in a ship called the *George*. (Select Cases in Chancery, 1364–1471—*Selden Society*, vol. x, p. 45.)

CHAPTER II

TOMB CHESTS AND WEEPERS

The practice of endowing chantry chapels enclosing the tomb, in which masses could be said for the soul of the deceased, had reached great proportions by the period with which we are dealing. In great abbeys or cathedrals these were sometimes placed between the pillars separating nave or choir from the aisles, a development from the great canopied tombs of Westminster and elsewhere. In smaller country churches chapels were sometimes formed by prolonging the nave aisles eastwards, as at Northleigh (1) or Ewelme. The tomb in such cases was usually placed in an arch opening into the chancel. In other cases a favourite situation was in the middle of the chancel in front of the altar, as at Arundel (6), but many of these have been moved in comparatively modern times as the incumbents have found them in the way. Many tombs are thus found pushed into odd corners, and in some cases robbed of much of their setting. Thus at Clifton (Beds) a table tomb (244) has been placed against the wall, and the little weepers of one side have had to be placed in the wall above the monument, and at Broughton a Lancastrian lady in SS collar of *c.* 1425 is now placed beside a Yorkist knight of some thirty years later. More modest monuments found a home in niches contrived in the walls of the church.

In many instances the effigies alone were of alabaster, and were placed on stone tombs; here it is only the complete alabaster monuments that will receive attention.

Mural tablets are very rare, only two belonging to our period being known. These are the Foljambe monument (1376) in Bakewell Church, with half-length figures of the knight and his lady set below a canopy as though looking out of a window (3), and a slab to Robert Gylbert at Youl-greave, Derbyshire, dated 1492, with a relief of Robert and his wife kneeling on either side of the Madonna, while seven sons kneel behind their father and nine daughters behind their mother (4).[1] The usual form consisted of a tomb chest surmounted by the effigy, or effigies, either set against the wall in an arched recess, or standing free in the shape of what is known as a table tomb. A tomb at Abergavenny (9) is a good example of the wall tomb, set in a recess beneath a depressed arch. In this case a special feature may be found in the alabaster reliefs set in the back of the recess. These are evidently the work of the retable workers referred to earlier, the central panel, representing the Assumption, being just one of the tall slabs used for the centrepiece of a reredos. As the tombs at Abergavenny are a collection from various places, one of which is said to be Tintern Abbey, it is difficult to know how far the various parts of these tombs belong to one another, but these reliefs appear to form part of a tomb, as there are two kneeling figures of a knight and his lady at the foot of the Virgin, which are more suitable for this purpose than for a reredos. On either side are slabs with kneeling figures and heraldic shields, and as the armour of these knights corresponds exactly with that of the knight at the foot of the central panel, as well as with that of the big effigy, it looks as though they had been rightly put together.

The table tombs may be illustrated by the very rich example at Norbury (10). Full-length figures of the knight and his lady rest on the tomb, while the sides of the tomb chest are divided up by a series of buttresses and canopies, or 'taber-

---

[1] A somewhat similar scene occupies the whole side of the tomb of Julian Nethermyl (d. 1539) at Coventry. This is a plain table tomb without effigies, and shows strong Flemish influence. It was no doubt provided by the Burton alabaster men, or possibly by a Fleming working for them.

nacles' as they were called, forming niches in which are placed a row of little figures, technically known as 'weepers'. Lofty canopies or arches were often erected over the tombs, and they were sometimes protected by iron grates.

The earliest tombs, such as those of John of Eltham (11, 12, 13) in Westminster Abbey and of Edward II at Gloucester (118), are composed of varied materials, and in the former the weepers are cut out and set against a background of dark-coloured composition.[1] In some other cases a similar scheme may have accounted for the disappearance of these little figures. In the fourteenth-century all-alabaster tombs the usual plan is to arrange the weepers under a continuous arcade of a comparatively simple character: the inner orders of the niche so formed are cusped, forming usually a cinque-foiled head, as at Warwick (29), or trefoiled as at Haversham (43). About the year 1400, when there was great activity in the alabaster shops, there was a good deal of variety. In some cases, as at Swine (14) or Harewood (15), angels are carved on the sides of the tomb chest without any niches. They usually hold shields, once blazoned with the arms of the deceased, or his family and connexions, and the ends of the tomb are usually occupied by a pair of them supporting the shield between them. A late example of these plain-background tombs is to be found at Macclesfield (66). It has been suggested above (p. 6) that these, like the curious seated angels at Methley (18) and Harewood (17), might perhaps be attributed to the York workshops. At Merevale (21) the angels are simply separated by little buttresses, and in other cases, as at Ashwell-thorpe, Bottesford (20) and Strelley, they are placed in plain square or oblong sunk panels.

At Lowick the contract already quoted stipulates for

---

[1] Recent cleaning at the abbey has revealed the fact that this dark background is not composed of black marble, or 'touch' as it is called, but of some kind of mastic, or dark plaster.

'tabernacles' over the heads of the angels; these are flat ogee canopies very like those fitted to the reredos 'tables'. The tomb of a priest at Wells (32, 47) has triple-headed canopies, separated by panels with shields.

In the second quarter of the century a rather formal system of panelling was introduced, resembling the tracery of a four- or six-light perpendicular window in two stages, as at Ashbourne (45) and Barmston (24). The angel or weeper figures occupy wider niches between the panels, or stand in square panels, as at Colne Priory. In very magnificent monuments, such as that of the Earl of Westmorland at Staindrop, the panels are complete models of little windows with arched heads, and the niches between them are richly carved, but in this case the weepers have unfortunately been destroyed. In one tomb from Colne Priory (30) of the end of the four-teenth century, the weepers are grouped in pairs beneath broad ogee canopies, a method which does not again become common till the end of the following century.

In the second half of the fifteenth century the usual scheme for an elaborate tomb is that followed at Norbury (10, 44) with ogee-headed niches capped by a foliage finial, separated by buttresses. Sometimes a double-headed niche is formed, with the central support omitted, and ending in a kind of pendant, as at Ewelme (28), and Aldermaston (277). This enabled the later carvers to introduce groups of two or three weepers into each niche, as at Ashover (61, 69), and these lead on into the transitional sixteenth-century groups with details of a Flemish renaissance type, like those at Kinlet (62). In some of these early sixteenth-century tombs the niches are round-headed and coarse, though still clumsily foiled, as at Castle Donington or Ross (52). In one or two other cases, as in one of the Vernon tombs at Tong (25, 36) and the Smythe tomb at Elford (26), the sides are most elaborately carved with an almost flamboyant kind of tracery, and have only a few small figures introduced at intervals standing in niches with vaulting ribs represented under the projecting canopies. In some of the latest examples, as at Aldermaston, spiral columns are introduced at the corners (57).

At all periods plainer tomb chests occur without weepers, sometimes decorated with niches, or with simple panelling, or heraldic devices as in the fine fourteenth-century tomb at Layer Marney (23). At the end of our period lozenge-shaped cusped panels containing shields become very common, and they seem to have been turned out by the dozen with very little variation. Good examples can be found at Holme Pierrepont and Ratcliffe-on-Soar (77) and another in the tomb of the Earl of Wiltshire at Lowick (209). In the south-west Purbeck marble tombs, sometimes with canopies as at Melbury Sampford and Puddletown, came into fashion again c. 1470, and later they spread over the Midlands as at Turvey, Beds. In this last the cusped lozenge pattern and spiral corner columns are reproduced in the darker material, which sets off the alabaster figures on the top.[1]

The weepers may be divided into three categories, angels, relatives of the deceased, and saints. Throughout our period the angel motive is very common. On the tombs they usually carry shields once blazoned with heraldry though in most cases the colours have faded or peeled off. Sometimes they have been refreshed in modern times, and so may easily prove dangerous traps for unwary genealogists. Occasionally, as at Dodford (27), the arms are carved in relief. In this last instance the angels at the end of the tomb kneel on either side of the shield. Some of the earlier angels are bare-headed, as

---

[1] Mr C. C. Oman has drawn my attention to some angels from a fifteenth-century tomb at Pembroke St Mary's, which have been reversed, and the back used to form a mural tablet to William Adams, 1603. There are a good many instances of palimpsest brasses, and it is interesting to have this alabaster example to put beside them.

at Bottesford (20), but later they usually wear a kind of low mitre, as at Dodford (27), Merevale (21) and elsewhere. These mitres have a small peak in front surmounted by a cross: at Willoughby-in-the-Wolds (16) the cross is taller and appears to rise from the crown behind the frontal peak.

The tips of the upper feathers are often turned up sharply as at Lowick (19) and Ashbourne (22). This might be a special trick of certain workshops like that at Chellaston, where the Lowick tomb was made, but they are so common that it is not safe to build too definite a theory on this practice. Angels are usually clad in an alb or surplice, but occasionally, as at Ewelme (28), they alternately wear albs and a kind of feathered tights, like the great wooden roof angels of the Eastern Counties. As this is the tomb of the Duchess of Suffolk and other details of the chapel have a resemblance to Eastern County work, there may be some connexion between these angels and the Norfolk and Suffolk work. Prof. Prior has suggested that the feathered tights were the costumes worn by angels in the mystery plays, from which the sculptors draw some of their inspiration. In the later examples the hair is brushed up round the cap or mitre in such a way as to look from a distance almost like a brim to a hat. This is seen beginning at Lowick (19) and in a more extreme form at Ashbourne (22).

The commonest use of weepers was to represent the family, or relations of the deceased. It had long been the custom to place figures of sons and daughters on the tomb chests, as in the case of the bronze statuettes on Edward III's tomb at Westminster, and of the earlier freestone tombs in the abbey. The motive was naturally taken up by the alabaster carvers. The actual family of the deceased is no doubt sometimes represented, but usually we should take these figures to be merely relatives, retainers or dependents, as it would be difficult always to produce the exact number of sons or daughters to fill the niches. In the tomb of Sir Nicholas Fitzherbert at

Norbury his two wives are not represented by large effigies on the top of the tomb, but appear to be introduced in the two figures at the end of the tomb, the survivor being dressed as a widow (46). In the case of the priest at Wells, small figures of canons appear in quire habit on the sides of the tomb chest (32), and friars or bedesmen sometimes occur when the great man commemorated had founded a chantry or hospital, as at Arundel (6) or North Aston (34). All these figures are most useful examples of the dress of the time,[1] and it is interesting to trace the development both of treatment and costume from the elegant king at Westminster with his slightly affected pose and exaggerated detail (31), through the richly-clad gentlemen and rather grim ladies of Warwick (29, 33, 37) to the graceful ladies of Elford (38) and the gorgeous armour and cloaks of Norbury (35, 44), and finally to the Tudor youth at Tong (36) and the varied head-dresses of the dames at Windsor, Aldermaston and Kinlet (40, 41, 42). The least attractive work is perhaps that of about 1470 or 1480, but beautiful figures are sometimes found, as at Ryther (56), and with the early sixteenth century there is a fresh refinement of detail and an attempt to vary the attitudes as at Fawsley (58, 60) or Windsor (59). At Aldermaston one of the weepers has his legs crossed as though about to walk away (277). At Stanford-on-Teme the sons are kneeling over their shields, and there is a group of three daughters on the end of the tomb (65). At Ashover (61) the shields have become mere heraldic emblems, and the weepers stand in groups of twos and threes sometimes holding one another by the hand. At Kinlet, with the first breath of the Renaissance (62), we have added refinement and an attempt to show the young warriors in attitudes indicative of grief, though the style of armour and accessories is just the same as that of the previous fifty years.

---

[1] For a fuller description of costumes, etc., see the following chapter, where the big effigies are classified and dated.

As the tombs were made by the same men who were engaged upon the retables it is natural to find saints or biblical scenes introduced among the weepers. Figures like the St Margaret (49) at Minster Lovell might do duty as part of a reredos. In some way too the sculptor, or rather those from whom he took his instructions, might have felt that he was putting the deceased under the protection of his favourite saints by placing their images on the tomb. Thus we find the Madonna at Abergavenny (51) and Minster Lovell, St Luke at Berkeley (50), St Christopher at Beaumaris, Minster Lovell, Harewood, etc. and at Ross St Anne teaching the young Virgin to read (52). A tomb at Harewood, c. 1490, has a very interesting set of saints, including St Laurence with his gridiron, Edward the Confessor with his ring, and St Stephen holding a pile of stones in his hand and others on his head (53, 54). Burton Agnes (Yorks) also has a good series, of which we illustrate St Anne and St Catharine (55). These saints are frequently ranged alternately with angels, as at Ross and Tong. At Abergavenny there are a number of figures holding scrolls, who appear to be prophets (48). Scenes are also introduced, the most common being the Annunciation, as at Wells (47), where again we notice the close correspondence to the work of the retable makers, and the same scene occupies the end of a tomb at Abergavenny with censing angels on each side (80). If it had not been for the square shape necessary for its position this last panel might have come straight from a reredos. Sometimes in this scene the angel and the Virgin occupy the opposite ends of the tomb chest, with the ordinary weepers arranged between them, as at Kinlet, and in the late example at Ross on the monument to Judge Rudhall (d. 1529), the judge, his wife and family are all kneeling behind the angel, as though taking part in the proceedings (63).

Sometimes, especially in the later tombs, the deceased and

his wife are introduced kneeling among the angels (Maccles-field) or saints as at Ashover (69). At Millom little kneeling figures are placed on each side of the angels (71).

Besides the tomb of Edward III's children in Westminster Abbey (74) there are a number of small monuments, which may be those of children or possibly were made to contain the heart only, the rest of the body being buried elsewhere. The effigy of a boy at Haccombe (75) obviously represents a child, but the small figure at Youlgreave (76) is in full armour and might represent an older boy. A tomb at Bakewell has no effigy, but the bedesmen placed round it as weepers do not suggest a child's monument (241).

The gruesome idea of having a decaying corpse, or cadaver, under the richly clad effigy of the deceased raised on a kind of table above, was sometimes employed in the fifteenth century, as at Ewelme, Arundel and under Bishop Beckyngton at Wells, but these horrible sculptures were not executed in alabaster and so need not be illustrated here.

CHAPTER III

THE EFFIGIES

When we come to deal with the effigies themselves there are one or two pitfalls to be avoided, and before attempting a classification of the figures a few general remarks will not be out of place. In the first place the popular identifications, and the labels often placed on the tombs, must be accepted with extreme caution. Inscriptions are rare before the latter part of our period, and as the heraldry was mainly added in colour which has perished, there is often considerable doubt as to the identity of the persons commemorated. Even where shields of arms still exist they often indicate little more than the family to which the deceased belonged, and we have to fall back upon the style of the costume and armour to find out whether we are dealing with father, son or grandson. Perhaps the crest, or badge worn on the helm upon which the head usually rests, except in some of the earlier examples, is a rather safer guide (108, 111). Unfortunately, however, this is frequently broken off. Different families, too, seem to have adopted the same or very similar badges at different periods, and like the titles borne by their owners these were sometimes conveyed by marriage with an heiress without conforming to the strict rules of heredity and succession which later came into force. Thus the Hiltons of Swine bear the chaplet of Lascelles derived from their mother (144, 159), and retain it for more than one generation. In a similar way Warwick the 'kingmaker' derived his earldom from marriage with Anne, daughter of Richard Beauchamp, Earl of Warwick. In the case of very well-known people, such as kings, princes and bishops, the names given in the guide-books are, no doubt, mostly correct, but in many other instances it is unsafe to accept the traditional identifications, or the labels affixed by local antiquaries of a previous generation, without much further investigation than is possible for anyone engaged on a general description like this. No doubt a great many of the names given are correct. If, for instance, a knight in the costume and armour of a certain period bears the arms of a certain family and is in a church adjoining that family's ancestral seat, there could not be many claimants to the monument. If, in addition, he wears the insignia of a distinctive order like that of the Garter the attribution becomes a practical certainty.

To check all these would demand an amount of local knowledge and historic research which only a highly specialised genealogist could supply, and the question arises whether it would not be safer to omit the names altogether. Personal connexions, however, add so much to the human interest that we can take in a monument that it is difficult to do otherwise than retain the traditional names, except in cases where the style of costume and armour shows them to be certainly wrong; but when these names are used here they must be taken as employed without absolute guarantee of their accuracy.

It must also be remembered that tombs were not always erected at the time of the death of the individual, but sometimes were prepared during his lifetime, and sometimes were not erected for years after his decease. Thus we know that the Lowick tomb was made within a year of Ralph Greene's death, but the bronze effigy of Richard Beauchamp, the great Earl of Warwick, who died in 1439 was not contracted for till 1450. In cases where husband and wife, or wives, were commemorated in the same monument, it might have been ordered on the death of any one of them, and where inscriptions are preserved, a blank space is sometimes left for the date of the death of one or other of the individuals represented, which has never been filled up. In disturbed times, too, such as those of the Wars of the Roses, which were going on for a great part of the alabaster period, many prominent men lost both their heads and their estates at the hands of the opposing faction, and it might be some time before a reverse of fortune enabled their descendants to pay the honours due to their ancestors.

PORTRAITURE

In seeking to identify the figures on the tombs with actual persons it must be borne in mind that portraiture, in the modern sense of the word, can hardly be said to have existed in medieval times. It is possible that here and there some attempt was made to conform to the general type of the person represented, especially in the case of kings or very great people, but the imagers seem to have paid far greater attention to costume and armour, to badges of rank or fashionable head-dress than to the actual features of the deceased. Katharine Greene the widow at Lowick orders a 'counterfeit of an esquire all armed for battle', and though minute directions are given for all details of the tomb, this is the only direction as to the individual representation of her husband. If we look through a series of photographs we cannot fail to notice how they all conform to the fashionable type of the period.

In the earlier tombs, at any rate, there seems to have been an idea that men liked to be represented at the perfect age— about 33—as they hoped to appear at the General Resurrection, and thus indications of age necessary for a real portrait would have been absent. Edward II at Gloucester (122) must thus be regarded as the ideal representation of a king, just as the statues and bronze effigy of Queen Eleanor of the previous generation look more like the artist's ideal of womanhood, based on his practice in making statues of the Madonna. It is only towards the end of our period that wrinkles and signs of old age begin to appear. Bishop Beckyngton of Wells, who died in 1465, is given some appearance of age (194), and occasionally a bald head like that of the knight at Ash, Kent (216) seems to suggest some approach to a general likeness.[1]

Some of the later effigies of the end of the fifteenth and early sixteenth centuries have an individual treatment which may be an attempt at portraiture, as in the Duke of Suffolk at Wingfield (275) or the priest in St Mary Redcliffe at Bristol (291), but these instances almost exhaust the list, and speaking generally it would be rash to try to ascertain the actual features of historic personages by examining their tombs, even if some sort of approximation to the general type of the deceased may sometimes have been in the sculptor's mind. Even the Bristol priest, which has such a strong appearance of individuality, may be only a type favoured by a particular sculptor; this is rather suggested by a comparison with the face of the judge at Yatton (292), not very far off, which bears a strong family likeness to the Bristol figure (see p. 80).

In the stone tomb at Hurstmonceux as late as the reign of Henry VIII Lord Dacre and his son lie side by side and the two effigies are exactly alike in feature as in armour. This cannot be merely due to a family likeness, but the sculptor must have been given an order for a couple of knightly effigies and saved himself trouble by making the second a replica of the first.

Where the greater part of the face was covered by the bascinet, or helmet, and the camail or gorget, protecting the neck, as in most of the earlier figures, little beyond eyes and nose or perhaps a moustache can appear, and little room is left for portraiture. By the middle of the fifteenth century

---

[1] The so-called judge at Willoughby-in-the-Wolds is also given a bald head, but this part of the effigy appears to have been patched, and may not be quite reliable.

the knights at Tong (181) or Dennington (176) are given a
bare upper lip, and would appear to have been clean-shaven
like the bare-headed knights of the succeeding generation.
Henry IV (182) and Sir Robert Waterton at Methley (90)
are among the latest of the bearded figures.

It is possible that the king would set the fashion of hair-
dressing and general type of face to which all his distinguished
subjects liked to conform. Thus Henry V was clean-shaven,
probably finding a beard inconvenient under a helmet;
from his time onward moustache and beard are rare, and
hair is worn short until Henry VII introduced the fashion of
wearing it down to his shoulders, while beards do not re-
appear till the days of Henry VIII. The first bearded knight
of the sixteenth century is probably Thomas Essex in St
Michael's, Coventry (286). Here and there more attention
has been given to the actual features, as in the bronzes of
Edward III and Richard II at Westminster, and the alabaster
head of Henry IV at Canterbury (182) certainly suggests a
portrait, bringing out a strange resemblance to his distant
successor Edward VII, but in the ordinary tombs little more
seems attempted than an approximation to a suitable type
for the person represented. Even the bronze effigy of so
famous a man as Richard Beauchamp, Earl of Warwick,
which at first glance seems to suggest rather individual
features, cannot have been modelled from his own appearance
as it was not ordered till 1450, eleven years after his death.[1]
The greatest care, however, was lavished upon his splendid
suit of Milanese armour, which was probably lent to William
Austen, the founder, to copy.

In the late effigy of Sir William Fielding at Monks' Kirby
(d. 1547, but the tomb probably erected during his lifetime),
there is a line across his forehead suggesting that the hair was

---

[1] The contract for the tomb chest was only made in 1454, which suggests
even longer delay before completion.

first carved in the usual way and later cut back to indicate his increasing baldness. We may regard this perhaps as an attempt at portraiture.[1]

SYMBOLS OF RANK

Symbols of rank, as stated above, were of much greater importance than personal features. Kings, princes, earls and dukes wear crown or coronet, and bishops and abbots their mitre and full mass vestments in accordance with their position. Towards the end of our period some priests are represented in cope or quire habit. Ladies of noble families also assert their rank by wearing coronet or knightly collar. Thus Isabella Nevill, niece of the Kingmaker, who is represented on the tomb at Elford as second wife of Sir William Smythe, in her glittering coronet (179, 256) completely outshines her predecessor, who lies on the other side of her husband. Knights of the Garter are represented in their robes towards the end of our period, the rich cloak, embroidered with the symbol of the order on the left shoulder, being worn over the armour, as by the Duke of Suffolk at Wingfield (275) or Sir John Cheyney at Salisbury (266). Lord Willoughby de Broke (d. 1503) at Callington, Cornwall (83) not only wears the collar and robe and the Garter, but has the Garter with its motto ('Honi soit qui mal y pense') repeated several times on the tomb chest, where it encircles his shield of arms. In earlier cases there was no robe, and we find the Garter merely strapped below the left knee, as shown in the Duke of Somerset at Wimborne (81) or Lord Bardolf at Dennington (176). In the rare instances where this order was conferred upon a woman it was worn on the left wrist, as at Ewelme by the Duchess of Suffolk (82): Lady Harcourt at Stanton Harcourt (177) wears it above the elbow.

More decorative still were the elaborate collars worn by

---

[1] Chatwin, *Birm. Arch. Soc. Transactions*, 1922.

knights and ladies of rank. The most important is that known as the SS collar. The origin and meaning of this famous decoration are lost in obscurity and have offered a wide field for conjecture. There seems to be little doubt that it was a livery collar of the House of Lancaster and was probably instituted by John of Gaunt. A drawing in the British Museum from a window in old St Paul's shows the arms of John of Gaunt within a collar of SS.[1] Mr Oswald Barron, F.S.A., writing in the eleventh edition of the *Encyclopaedia Britannica*, refers to a complaint by the Earl of Arundel before Parliament in 1394 that Richard II was wont to wear the livery of the collar of the Duke of Lancaster, his uncle, and that people of the king's following wore the same livery. The king replied that after his uncle's return from Spain in 1389, he himself took the collar from the duke's neck, and put it on his own, which collar the king would wear and use for a sign of the good and whole-hearted love between them. The late Dean of York quotes Gower's *Vox Clamantis* (1387), where Henry of Lancaster is referred to 'qui gerit S', and a wardrobe account of Henry in 1391–2 in which figures the item: 'Pro I colu auri facto pro domino Henrico Lancastrie, comite Derb. cum xxii literis de S.' In 1401 a statute was passed granting permission to all sons of the king, and to dukes, earls, barons and lesser barons, to 'use the livery of our lord the king of his collar as well in his absence as in his presence, and to knights and esquires in his presence only'.[2] There can be little doubt that this collar came into general use among the most distinguished adherents of the Lancastrian cause with the accession of Henry IV in 1399, and it was worn by women as well as men. It would be a useful guide in dating effigies if we could say that it was not used before that date, but there are a few cases that appear to be earlier, and the wearers

---

[1] Hartshorne, *Recumbent Effigies in Northamptonshire*.
[2] See also A. Hartshorne on the SS collar, *Arch. Journ.* vol. xxxix.

would then seem to have been specially attached to the household of John of Gaunt. The earliest instance at present known is the collar of an effigy at Spratton, Northants (143), which is identified by the heraldry as Sir John Swinford, who died in 1371. He was a follower of John of Gaunt, and even if a few years elapsed before the tomb was set up, the style of armour, etc., clearly belongs to the last quarter of the fourteenth century. Another early example is on the tomb attributed to Sir John Marmion, at Tanfield, who died in 1386, and here again the figure is distinctly fourteenth-century in style, even if it should be proved to belong to another member of the Marmion family. The effigy attributed to Sir Thomas de Arderne (d. 1391) at Elford (149) also has an SS collar, but this tomb may really be that of Sir John de Arderne, who died in 1408. In the earliest form of the collar the esses seem to have been of metal, usually laton, attached to a band of leather, or some such material. The letters were gilded and the band painted green. Good examples may be quoted from Ashwellthorpe (84, 85), Longford (86), and Staindrop (93). In some cases the letters are worked up into a more intricate pattern, as at Tong (181) or combined with a kind of metal chain, as at Harewood (92).

What the SS stands for is a matter of conjecture and has been a puzzle to generations of antiquaries. The suggestion that it stands for Henry IV's motto 'Soverayne', which is put forward by Stothard, seems disproved by its earlier use by John of Gaunt. That it stands for 'Senescallus', the office of steward of England having been bestowed on John of Gaunt, seems far-fetched. One attractive explanation is that offered by Mr H. B. McCall, F.S.A., in his *Richmondshire Churches*, where he suggests the origin to be a motto 'Soveine vous de moy', the forget-me-not having been a favourite flower of Henry IV before he became king. In 1397–8 Herman Goldsmith provided a collar 'cum esses et floribus de Souveigne vous de moy'. The statue of Henry V on the quire screen at York wears the SS collar, and a band across the breast bears the words 'Memento mei'. Figures of John Beaufort and his duchess in glass at Landbeach (Cambs) have beneath them the words 'Souvent me souvient'.

The obvious suggestion that the esses stand for 'Sanctus' obtains some confirmation from a reference to a collar of gold in John of Gaunt's will,[1] where he speaks of it as having the names of God written on each part of it. This might refer to the 'Sanctus, Sanctus, Sanctus', or alternatively to 'Salvator'. This particular collar is spoken of as having been given to John of Gaunt by his mother. Hartshorne says[2] that church vestments were not unfrequently powdered with esses for 'Sanctus'.

It is, of course, not impossible that the esses were merely a practical adaptation of a series of broken links of a chain, and had originally no more significance than the S-shaped buckles on the belts used to support the trousers of sportsmen at the end of the Victorian era, and that various meanings were suggested for them as these collars came into general use. This would have been quite in accordance with the ideas of medieval scholastic philosophy, which used the most extraordinary ingenuity to twist all phenomena of history and nature to a moral or prophetic significance.

The Yorkists, in their turn, introduced the collar of suns and roses, good examples of which occur at Norbury[3] (98,

---

[1] Extract from will of John of Gaunt, 1398: 'Je ly devise un fermail d'or del veil manere, et escript les noms de Dieu en chascun part de icel fermail, la quel ma treshonoré dame et miere la Roigne...me donna.'

[2] *Arch. Journ. loc. cit.* See also articles in *Proc. Soc. Antiq. Newcastle-on-Tyne*, 3rd ser. vol. VII (1916), nos. 16 (pp. 204, 223), and *Church of Our Fathers*, by Rev. D. Rock.

[3] The effigy of the Countess of Arundel, lady of Earl William who died in 1487, wears a collar on which the suns and roses are separated by oak leaves, the badge of the Fitzalans. (This is not illustrated here as the effigies are not of alabaster; but they are well drawn by Stothard.)

206), Harewood (94) and Holme Pierrepont (87). If Dr Cox is right in assigning this last tomb to Sir Henry Pierrepont, who died in 1499—and the armour is certainly late fifteenth-century in type—it shows that this collar could still be worn after the deposition of Richard III in 1485. The lady at Wethersfield (283) also appears to be after 1485. In a few instances during the reign of Henry VII an attempt was made to combine the York and Lancaster collars in a special Tudor collar formed of esses alternating with roses. A good example of this may be found at Harewood (95, 243). In the figure attributed to Sir Thomas Erdington at Aston (d. 1433), but evidently not made till thirty years later, the esses have been removed from the collar, which remains blank, suggesting family feuds or the changing of sides in those troublous times.

Henry VII restored the SS collar, and it again becomes common in his reign, the design being often elaborated and enriched, as at Elford (179) and Eye (254). In these later examples the collar was broader, and hangs down lower over the breast than in the earlier instances. These collars were valuable and prized possessions, and are specifically mentioned in wills as a special bequest, as in that of Sir John Darell in 1509.[1]

COLOUR

All the effigies were, of course, gorgeously coloured and gilded. Much of this decoration has perished; time has caused the colours to fade and restorers have often cleaned off what was left during well-meant but unfortunate repairs. Many traces, however, still remain to enable us to form some idea of what the original effect must have been like. Sometimes

---

[1] His effigy still exists in Little Chart Church, Kent (203). Mr Ralph Griffin, F.S.A., gives the extract from his will in *Archaeologia Cantiana*, vol. xxxvi (1923), pp. 139, 140: 'To Dame Anne my wif my coler of gold of esses'.

the whole was completely covered, even the faces receiving a flesh tint, but usually the faces and hands were polished, leaving the beautiful material to give the effect required. Sometimes larger surfaces seem to have been left plain, only jewellery, sword belts, and borders of garments being painted or gilded, and jewels of paste or glass were inserted when opportunity occurred.

A good idea of the colour scheme adopted may be gathered from Richardson's description of the tomb at Elford (149) which he restored with admirable skill, but rather more drastically than we should approve of now. Unfortunately in order to get rid of initials and abrasions he found it necessary to clean off the considerable traces of colour which still existed, but he recorded the following facts. The leaves of the coronet and ends of the plume of the helm, on which the head rests, were bordered and tipped with gold. The plume was red and borders of armour and details gilt. The ground of the SS collar was green and the letters and jewel gilt. The belt and handle of the sword were crimson and gold and fastenings gilt. There was no colour on the jupon except a gold border on the scalloping and waist fillet. The spurs were gilt, and the mane and tail of the lion were gold and his mouth red. The face and hands of the lady were flesh-colour, the lower cushion crimson, the upper green and the tassels gilt, green and white. The angels' hair and borders of dress were gilt. The lady's head-dress had gilt flowers and green leaves, her hair was brown, and her mantle blue, edged with gold and lined with red. Her collar was green with gilt SS. Her dress was brown and gold, lining green, kirtle crimson, sleeves white, fastenings gold. This description suggests the gorgeous effect these monuments must have produced. As few of the tombs preserve more than a faint suggestion of their original splendour we may best gain an idea of the style of the painting by looking at those alabaster altar panels in our museums which still preserve something of the rich colour effect, such as the complete reredos recently acquired by the Victoria and Albert Museum, South Kensington.

Stothard's careful drawings, made in the early years of the nineteenth century before restoration or the craze for scraping and cleaning up had set in, are a useful record of the colours of which he found traces surviving. Thus the effigy of the famous warrior Sir Hugh Calveley at Bunbury (156) had the jupon painted with the family arms (Argent, a fess gules between three calves sable). The helm on which his head rests was red with a black calf's head as crest, and a few other details were picked out in red. The embroidered band round the bascinet, the lion at his feet and the edges and ornamental details of the armour were gilded, the rest of the armour apparently being left in the natural white polished surface of the alabaster. The face was flesh colour, though in some other cases it would seem to have been left uncoloured.

Stothard shows a very similar scheme in the fine tomb at Ashwellthorpe (84, 85). In the knight the jupon and crest are brilliantly coloured, the sword belt is red and details of the chasings at the edges of the armour and spurs gilded. The orle round the bascinet is gold on green, and the SS collar is gold on a blue band. The lady's hair and ornaments are gilded, her skirt red and the lining of her cloak ermine.

Such descriptions leave the impression that the alabaster was more valued for its ease of working and fine detail than for the inherent beauty of the material, as so large a part of the surface was covered. Such a figure, however, as that of William of Wykeham at Winchester (162), where much of the colour is preserved, gives an impression of richness which does not entirely obscure the quality of the alabaster, and contrasts favourably with such a figure as Archbishop Chichele at Canterbury, which is so thickly covered with modern paint that one cannot see what it is made of.

POSTURE

The effigies are placed flat on their backs, and there is little variety in pose and attitude. We miss the differences of posture and expression of the stone effigies of the beginning of the fourteenth century, but with the introduction of plate armour easier attitudes would have been impossible. At any rate the English sculptors were not guilty of such a lapse from truth as the Italian artist who made the beautiful effigy of Guidarello Guidarelli at Ravenna, and who in order to obtain a sentimental expression turned the neck of his warrior to one side and in so doing bent the stiff steel gorget as though it had been soft leather! If the English figures are apt to become monotonous and conventional in comparison with their predecessors, they gain in richness of detail, and when finely well preserved give us a better idea of what a medieval tomb looked like, as the detail is carved in the soft alabaster, whereas in most of the freestone figures much of it was added in the gesso and colour which has failed to stand the test of time, and left these figures little more than the core of the finished article.

The tomb slab is usually moulded and projects beyond the chest, and the broader hollow moulding is sometimes filled by flowers or leaf-patterns placed at intervals. In some cases, especially in the later monuments, there are inscriptions in English, French or Latin giving the names and dates of the deceased, beginning ORATE PRO ANIMA, and usually ending in a prayer for their souls, the commonest formula being CUJUS ANIME PROPICIETUR DEUS, often in a contracted form (CUI AĪE PꝐICIETUR DEUS). When husband and wife lie together there is sometimes a gap left for the date of death of one or other, showing that the tomb was set up on the death of one but that the survivors of the second failed to complete the record. In a few cases an inscription might have been placed on a brass strip, but more often may have been painted and so perished, but they were not usual before the sixteenth century.[1] Earlier examples may be quoted from Ashton (Northants) MONSR JOHAN D' HERTESHULL GIST YCY DIEU DE SA AIME EYT MERCY AMEN (he died in 1365); and from Dodford, HIC JACET JOHĒS CRESSY MILES D'NUS ISTI VILLE QUONDAM CAPITANI DE LYCIEUX ORBEF ET PONTLEVEQUE IN NORMĀDIA ET CŌCILIARĪ DÑI REGIS IN FRANCIA QUI OBIIT APUD TOVE IN LOIRINA IIII° DIE MARCII ANNO DÑI M°CCCCXLIIII CUI ANĪE P̄PICIETUR DEUS AMEN.

The *gablettes* stipulated for in the Lowick contract are repeated, as already mentioned, in the tombs of Henry IV and Queen Joan at Canterbury and of the Earl and Countess of Arundel at Arundel (6). They are also found a few years later at Abergavenny, and with two ecclesiastics, Archbishop Stratford (d. 1348) at Canterbury and Bishop Stafford (d. 1419) at Exeter (197). A knight of fourteenth-century date at Greystoke, Cumberland, also has one of rather different shape faced with little shields (137), and the small effigy at Apethorpe (*c.* 1500) (79) described later on p. 76, has a group of the Coronation of the Virgin with attendant angels placed over the knight's head as a kind of substitute for a canopy.

The slab is frequently edged with a series of miniature battlements, as at Norbury (10, 46). At Spilsby there are a series of little figures in niches all round the slab, but these tombs have been so restored that this feature may not be relied on as original.

In double tombs husband and wife lie side by side, with the knight's head resting on his helm and the lady's on a cushion, the latter often supported by angels seated on the slab.

---

[1] The inscription cut on the tomb slab of a knight at Elford must be regarded with suspicion. This tomb was restored by Richardson and this identification was probably only his conjecture.

Cushions are usually double, with the upper one laid across the lower so that the corners do not coincide, and there are usually tassels at the corners. Civilians, like the ladies, have these cushions, and even knights have them instead of the helm occasionally. This is more usual in the earlier period, as at Westminster (11) or Meriden (157), but occurs spasmodically at all times, as at Salisbury (266), Ormskirk, Halsall or Bromham (284).

Even civilians occasionally rest their heads on a helm with its crest, as in the case of the Judge at Yatton (292), and Ralph Swillington, the Attorney General who died in 1525, at Coventry (286).

At Ashby-de-la-Zouch a figure dressed as a pilgrim (210), but whose noble birth is attested by the SS collar, rests on his broad-brimmed hat. In one or two cases angels are introduced beside the helm, as at Ash (216), and also at Elford (149) if Richardson's restoration is correct.

The little angels holding up the cushions are usually sitting or reclining on the slab (162, 236), and most of them are graceful figures clad in albs, though occasionally we find the feathered tights of the mystery plays, like those of the wooden angels of the East Anglian roofs; at Ewelme there are four of these to support the cushion of the Duchess of Suffolk (183).

In a few instances angels are introduced to hold up the helm of the knight, but this is not common. They occur at Elford (149) and Porlock.

The knight's feet usually rest on a lion (102) or some other beast, forming his badge or figuring in his arms. The lady usually rests hers on little dogs, who are sometimes playing with the folds of her skirt, giving a living and playful touch to relieve the monotony of the conventional attitude, e.g. at Arundel (101).

Bishops sometimes have a lion, like the knights, and Archbishop Langham (100) has delightful little dogs with bells round their collars. In a brass at Deerhurst the dog's name *Terri* is inscribed, and another at Ingham, now unhappily destroyed, had a dog named *Jakke*.[1]

Bishop Harewell at Wells (103) has two hares in a punning reference to his name.

The helm on which the knights rest their heads is the great tilting helm with its lofty crest, now unfortunately often broken off. The Saracen's head crest of Lord Cobham at Lingfield (111) and a similar example on the Duke of Suffolk's tomb at Wingfield (108) are good examples, as also the peacock of Lord Rous at Bottesford (204).

At Norbury a little figure of a bedesman is perched on the lion at the feet of the knight (106), and this idea is repeated in a number of later monuments, as in that of the Earl of Wiltshire at Lowick (105) and in the fine well-preserved tomb of a member of the Redman family at Harewood (107). In the last the little bedesman is used to hide the rather ugly sole of one of the clumsy sabatons which came into fashion towards the end of the fifteenth century, the other being supported by the well-curled tuft of the lion's tail. Lord Willoughby de Broke at Callington, in Cornwall, has two bedesmen, one supporting each foot. Bedesmen also occur at the feet of Sir George Manners at Windsor, Sir Giles Daubeny at Westminster, Sir John Strelley at Strelley and at Exton in Rutland. We have already noticed them on a larger scale among the weepers on the sides of the tomb chest (see p. 19). Probably in these cases where the bedesmen occur the deceased had been patron or founder of a chantry or hospital. In the great tomb of the Earl of Westmorland and his two wives at Staindrop, beyond the lions there is a series of little figures of clerks sitting on each side of a kind of

---

[1] Macklin, *Brasses of England*, pp. 160, 174.

lectern or reading desk, but unfortunately their heads and upper portions have been broken away, though their books are still open before them (104). The great Bishop William of Wykeham at Winchester has three monks seated at his feet (163): these might be taken as his secretaries or executors, or, more likely, representatives of his colleges at Winchester and Oxford.

Though almost all the stone knights of the late thirteenth and early fourteenth centuries have their legs crossed, there are only three or four known instances of this attitude in alabaster. No doubt this pose, comfortable enough in mail, would have been awkward in the plate armour of the succeeding period. With one or possibly two exceptions the cross-legged knights are all early, the figure at Hanbury (117) being no product of the regular alabaster craftsmen, whose shops were not established at his date; Prince John of Eltham at Westminster (119) is probably the work of London sculptors for whose use the alabaster had been imported in the rough, while the knight at Wantage may be a local production (129). The one late example is a much-mutilated knight at Burton-on-Trent, only recently moved from the open air into the local museum. It is in a terrible condition, but enough remains to show the attitude and to indicate a date of *c.* 1470, or even later. The shield at his side, which is also an almost unique feature at this date, is of a distinctly Tudor shape. It is strange that this solitary example of the cross-legged attitude should occur a hundred years later than any other known specimen.[1] In this connexion it may be worth while

---

[1] Mr P. B. Chatwin, F.S.A., has made a close examination of this figure, and has kindly sent me photographs of it, which certainly bear out the description and dating given in the text. A mutilated torso, little more than a lump of alabaster, is also preserved at Kingsbury, near Birmingham, which suggests that it may have been part of a knight lying on his side like the early fourteenth-century figures at Aldworth or Aber-

to mention that one of the weepers at Aldermaston, *c.* 1526, is standing with legs crossed in a lively attitude (277).

In the alabaster knights, with the exception of the first example at Hanbury, the earlier sword-drawing motif is definitely abandoned, and hands are almost always folded in prayer. Sometimes, however, husband and wife clasp hands, especially in the later fourteenth and early fifteenth centuries, as at Warwick (148), Elford (149), Strelley (150), Lowick (180), and Wimborne (81). In most cases the gauntlet is taken off and held in the left hand, in order to leave the right free to hold that of the lady, or else it is, placed on the slab beside the figure. Late examples occur, *c.* 1495, at Macclesfield (66) and Warrington (7).

Widows are usually modestly veiled, and wear a barbe, a kind of crimped veil, over the chin, as at Stourton Caundle (227), Haversham (152), Lingfield (116) and Harewood (114). In a few cases small figures of children are placed in the folds of the draperies at the side. At Kinlet there is an infant tightly wrapped in swaddling clothes (often described as a chrism child), indicating perhaps that the lady died in giving birth to the child (225). At Horwood two sons are placed on one side, and two daughters on the other (226), while at Stourton Caundle there is a whole column of little figures, one above another, too worn to be made out clearly, but apparently illustrating the same idea (227). At Burton Agnes a small figure of a son in full armour is placed on the slab beside his father, and another of a daughter beside her mother, both small figures being practically replicas on a reduced scale of the main effigies (221).

In dating effigies the chief criterion must be the costume and armour of the knights, and as inscriptions are rare until

---

gavenny, but so little is left that it is impossible to say whether the alabaster man here attempted to follow the designs of his freestone mason predecessors.

the end of our period we are much helped by the wonderful series of contemporary brasses, many of which have preserved their inscriptions. There are, however, one or two strange differences in the alabaster and brass treatment, which should be noticed. For instance, the orle, or jewelled chaplet worn round the bascinet, which is such a feature in the splendid alabasters of the first half of the fifteenth century, as at Dennington (176), Bromsgrove (91), and Tong (181), is very rare in the brasses. In the famous manuscript[1] illustrating the life of Richard Beauchamp, Earl of Warwick, the earl is described as entering a tournament with his bascinet decorated with a 'chapellet rich of perle & precious stones'. Froissart describes a scene in which Edward III gave a chaplet of pearls to the gallant French knight Sir Eustace de Ribeaumont as a token of his admiration for the valour shown by this adversary.

This chaplet or orle was a very decorative feature and was eagerly seized upon by the alabaster carvers as giving an opportunity to make the most of their fine-grained material. In the second half of the fifteenth century great ladies frequently wore their hair loose and simply encircled by a coronet as at Elford (179) or Lockington (268): when they had not the necessary qualification for a coronet they sometimes substituted a kind of orle, as at Turvey, Thurlaston (260) or Batley (261). It occurs also in an exaggerated form on the head of Sir Robert Waterton at Methley (90), where he is represented in armour, but without the usual bascinet found at his date (1424). In this case a kind of orle is substituted, and is very large and richly carved, looking like a sort of turban. Here we have, perhaps, a very gorgeous form of the chaperon, the fashionable civilian hat of the first half of the fifteenth century. It consisted of a roundlet, something like a small inflated motor tyre, with a broad piece of cloth called a *gorget* attached to it, which could be draped round the neck or

---

[1] Published by Viscount Dillon and W. H. St John Hope, Longmans Green and Co. 1914.

thrown over the shoulder, and a narrower strap-like tail called a *liripipe* by which the whole could be balanced when thrown backwards. This type of head-dress is shown in the civilian effigies at Harlaxton and Aston-on-Trent (151), and is even better shown in the weepers on the tomb at Haversham (43).

The differences between the brass treatment and that of the alabasters is perhaps most marked in the transitional period between the camail and jupon knights and that of the fully developed plate armour—our period III in the following classification. Besides the rarity of the orle[1] in the brasses already mentioned, there are quite a number of differences. For instance, figures wearing the skirt of overlapping hoop-like plates without the tassets (i.e. the pointed pendant plates bolted on to the fauld, and protecting the thighs) are much commoner in the brasses than in the alabasters. In the brasses too the shoulders are protected by roundels, or circular palettes in nearly every case, while in the effigies in the round such plates are commonly omitted, or when introduced are of all kinds of shapes.[2] The elaborately embossed hip-belt also lasts longer in the alabasters than in the brasses, perhaps because it afforded an opportunity for the rich decoration beloved of the Nottingham carvers. It is retained as an ornament, or merely to support the misericorde, or dagger, long after it had been superseded by the diagonal bawdric, or sword belt (see p. 49 below), though both belts do not occur together on the brasses. Very often in the latter the misericorde is simply laid beside the knight without any apparent support. These differences are probably due mainly to the differing technique required for the metal and the alabaster. A simpler scheme was desirable in the brasses

---

[1] The orle occurs in brasses at Lingfield, Spilsby and Harpham. I am indebted to the late Mr F. E. Howard for drawing my attention to several of these points in this comparison between the alabasters and brasses.

[2] Round ones occur in the two earliest knights at Harewood (92), at Wootton Wawen (168) and at Methley (90).

which were more or less outline drawings, and the engravers shirked the delicate detail so effective in the alabaster.

It is also difficult to recognise in the alabasters the famous butterfly head-dress of the brasses. This is partly because a more restrained treatment is necessitated by the recumbent position, with the head resting on a pillow. The science of perspective, too, was evidently not quite mastered by the makers of the brasses, and it is difficult to see exactly what they intended to represent. Probably, therefore, the alabaster version in the round gives a more accurate idea of what was actually worn, and the student of costume should therefore turn to such effigies as those at Ilton (229), Methley (223), Norbury (237), London (242), or Marnhull (233), rather than to the brasses for information, though the brasses attempt to give the effect of the fluttering kerchief hanging down behind, which in the alabasters has to be folded back, or spread flat over the cushion.

The *hennin*, or tall steeple head-dress, seems to have been a French, and specially a Burgundian fashion, and does not appear on English monuments, unless the very truncated form worn by the lady at South Cowton (115) may be regarded as a modification of it.

The strange, and rather ghastly, shrouded effigies at Fenny Bentley (298) are all assigned to members of the Beresford family who died between 1470 and 1480. The ends of the shrouds are tied above the heads and below the feet, allowing nothing but the general shape of the corpse to appear beneath the wrappings. Such a morbid idea would be more in place in the sixteenth century than the fifteenth, and if the attribution is correct they may have been set up posthumously.[1]

---

[1] A brass of this type, however, dating from 1484 is illustrated in the V. & A. Museum *List of Rubbings of Brasses*, published in 1915. Macklin also gives a number of brasses ranging from 1431 to 1660, but commoner in the later periods (*Brasses of England*, p. 211).

CHAPTER IV

CLASSIFICATION OF THE EFFIGIES

Recumbent effigies may be divided into those of kings, civilians, knights, ladies and ecclesiastics, but, as already stated, the armour of the knights is the most distinctive feature upon which classification can be based, and it will be convenient to let the others fall into their places beside the knights. The head-dresses of the ladies follow a course of evolution more or less parallel to that of the armour of their husbands, but the ecclesiastics are more constant to type throughout the period. Mass vestments are very much the same all through and it is much more difficult to date a bishop or priest than any other personage, as we have to judge merely by subtle differences of style and treatment. In a few instances towards the end of our period the quire habit is worn, as in the figure of John Bothe, Prebendary of Lichfield, at Sawley (128).

The earliest bishops, such as Archbishop Stratford at Canterbury, d. 1348 (184), or Bishop Hatfield at Durham, d. 1381 (124), still retain something of the free experimental style of the earlier fourteenth-century types. Later the treatment tends to become more dry and linear, as in Abbot Seabroke (d. 1457) at Gloucester (127); while towards the end of our period there is a tendency to a more individual treatment of feature that we have already noticed in the priest at Bristol (291).

The classification here adopted is according to date, and the alabaster effigies may be roughly divided into six categories. These may overlap slightly, and there are some transitional figures, while time naturally brought some development from the earlier to the later examples of the same category. On the whole, however, as the main centres of production seem to have been near together, in the neighbourhood of Nottingham and Burton, new styles were quickly adopted in all the workshops, and such overlappings would not be for more than a few years.

The five main divisions are as follows: (i) early experiments before 1360; (ii) the Edwardian, from 1360 to about 1420; (iii) the Lancastrian, from about 1415 to 1450; (iv) the Yorkist, from about 1440 to 1485; (v) the Early Tudor, from 1480 to 1530 or 1540. To these it may be useful to add a sixth (vi) to include a few specimens which retain Gothic characteristics after the main stream of production had been directed into Renaissance channels under Italian, and still more under Flemish influences. In this last category no attempt has been made at a comprehensive survey as in the others. The break at the Reformation was less sharp in monuments than in any other branch of architectural art, but the years 1534–40 which include the Act of Supremacy and the dissolution of the monasteries seem to be the most appropriate time at which to draw a line to mark the end of medieval England. It also corresponds roughly with the time when the old native Gothic art was rapidly giving place to foreign ideas and to Ruskin's 'foul torrent of the Renaissance'.

The labels given in the above classification are not strictly accurate, as the Lancastrian dynasty was in power long before 1415, and the Yorkist before 1440, and it would perhaps be better to name them after the most characteristic features of the armour. Thus we might call (ii) the camail (or aventail) and jupon period, (iii) the first complete plate, and (iv) that of the elaborated and fluted plate armour. Modern authorities would probably prefer to drop the dynastic labels as misleading, but they are short and convenient and are retained here for the sake of clarity. Recent research also rejects many of the names attached to the various portions of armour by the older writers on this subject, and thus the way of the commentator is full of pitfalls. The name 'Gothic armour' has traditionally become attached to that of our last two periods only, presumably because writers have approached the subject from the point of view of collectors of the surviving suits of armour, which are extremely rare in the transitional period from mail to plate, and have only turned to the effigies in the second place, for their examples.

PERIOD I

EARLY EXPERIMENTS BEFORE 1360

The earliest known alabaster effigy is that at Hanbury, near the Tutbury quarries, attributed to Sir John de Hanbury who died in 1303 (117). It is a cross-legged figure in mail and surcoat, with shield on the left arm and drawing the sword from the scabbard, just in the manner of the freestone knights that were being produced all over England *c.* 1300. The alabaster is of the brownish streaky variety, not the pure white kind which was mostly in use till the end of the Gothic period, and this tomb is evidently the work of the usual monumental masons experimenting in the local stone.

As already pointed out (p. 3), the first sign of the discovery of the suitability of alabaster for tombs may be found in its employment for a group of royal monuments in the first half of Edward III's reign. A magnificent monument was erected to Edward II (118) at Gloucester, consisting of an alabaster figure of the king, resting on a Purbeck marble tomb under an elaborate freestone canopy, and this mixed construction suggests the idea that it was the work of the royal masons. Prof. Lethaby mentions several Gloucester masons as working for the king at Westminster at about this time, and, as London has no building-stone of its own, the London sculptors would have been used to working in varied materials imported from elsewhere. The head of Edward II

(122) is of an ideal type, belonging to the early fourteenth century, and, though it may have been somewhat touched up when the canopy was mended, the face is strikingly beautiful. The head is supported by angels in the Westminster manner of the preceding period.

Another early alabaster is to be found on the tomb of Prince John of Eltham, son of Edward II, who died in 1334, and was buried at Westminster (11, 12, 13, 119). Here again we have seen that the tomb is of mixed materials, effigy and weepers being of alabaster, but the weepers are set against a background of dark composition. The splendid canopy has disappeared, though drawings[1] of it still exist. The effigy is the direct successor of the royal tombs of the sanctuary. The prince lies with his head supported by angels and legs crossed, and wears that kind of surcoat[2] cut short in front, worn only at about this period. Here again we are probably justified in assuming a London origin, the alabaster having been imported in the rough.

Prince William of Hatfield, second son of Edward III, who died about 1346 when quite a young boy, has a very pleasing, though much worn effigy, about 4 ft. 6 in. long at York (120). It is a valuable example of the costume of a noble youth of the period, and the elaborate embroideries of the tunic, and borders of the cloak, gave the sculptor an opportunity of making use of the qualities of his beautiful material.

A small tomb of alabaster was also erected at Westminster to two children of Edward III. They are represented as at least ten years old (74) and are dressed almost as if of mature age, though they died when quite infants: this is evidence that portraiture as we know it was hardly taken seriously at

---

[1] Illustrated by Crossley in *English Church Monuments*, p. 57.
[2] This type of surcoat is called a *cyclas* by older writers, but there is now said to be no foundation for the use of the term to denote this particular form of it.

this time. John Orchard, who supplied this tomb (see p. 7) was also employed on that of Queen Philippa, but her own effigy was made by Hawkin Liège, a Frenchman, and so hardly comes within our list of English monuments. It also appears to be of white marble, and not of alabaster, as it has usually been described, and so comes definitely outside the scope of this article.[1]

Archbishop Stratford at Canterbury, who died in 1348 (184), is probably our earliest ecclesiastic in alabaster. Though somewhat mutilated the effigy is also the best as a work of art. The face was delicately rendered and the folds of the chasuble are arranged with consummate skill and variety, details of the stole and other ornaments being elaborately chased. Prof. Prior was of opinion that the earlier alabaster bishops, like the princes, came from London, or, at any rate, were of Westminster inspiration, indicating an origin of the trade in the royal workshop, from which it spread to Nottingham and places like Chellaston in the immediate neighbourhood of the quarries, which thenceforth became the chief centre of manufacture. Bishop Hatfield of Durham (124) has the elaborate embroideries of the York prince (120), and the Durham accounts mention the importation of marble and alabaster from London in 1372 and 1380.[2] Bishop Ralph at Wells, d. 1363, whose effigy should by its date be placed in our next section (191), has considerable likeness in general treatment to Archbishop Stratford. This effigy, too, has a strong resemblance to the stone figure of Bishop Sheppey of Rochester (d. 1360), which would presumably be of London work.

Of the first knights in armour belonging to this period the

---

[1] Prof. Prior was the first to draw my attention to this point. His opinion is now confirmed by the Royal Commission on Historical Monuments, in their sumptuous volume on *Westminster Abbey*, 1924.

[2] See p. 8.

most important is Sir Hugh Despenser at Tewkesbury, d. 1349 (123), who lies with his lady beneath a superb canopy of the Gloucester type. He wears a round-topped bascinet, and over the mail a tight-fitting jupon of leather, while his wife wears the sideless *côte-hardi* with large buttons down the front and the extraordinary square-framed head-dress in fashion at the time, composed of a series of little frills. This is sometimes called the *nebule* or *nebuly* head-dress.

Two tombs assigned to knights who died in the 'sixties are of early form and may be included in our first division. They are those assigned to Sir William Fitzwarren at Wantage (129) (d. 1361) who still has the crossed legs of the previous period, and Sir John de Herteshull (130) at Ashton, Northants (d. 1365), whose memorial inscription has already been quoted (p. 35). Both wear the camail, the curtain of mail suspended from the bascinet to protect the neck, which is the distinguishing feature of our next class, but it is treated in a tentative manner in these transitional figures.

PERIOD II

THE EDWARDIAN OR CAMAIL AND JUPON, 1360–1420

This is also known as the camail and jupon period, from these distinctive features which occur throughout till superseded by the plate armour of the next class. The camail, or aventail as it was usually called in England, is the curtain of mail suspended from the helmet and falling over the shoulders, protecting the neck; the jupon, or 'gipon' as Messrs Kelly and Schwabe prefer to spell it, takes the place of the long linen surcoat, and assumes the form of a smooth leather garment without sleeves, descending below the waist, as shown in the Despenser monument referred to above. Arms and legs are protected by plate armour, and small roundels of steel begin to be used to protect the joints on shoulder and elbow. The jupon was often fringed or scalloped at the bottom, and was no doubt painted with the arms of the wearer. The latter are only occasionally worked in relief, but in all cases must have been brilliantly coloured.

From the shape of this garment, which in a number of instances, e.g. the tombs of Thomas Beauchamp at Warwick (148) or the Arderne knight at Elford (149), swells out over the breast, it looks as though a metal breastplate were worn underneath, as well as the 'haubergeon', or shirt of mail, portions of which appear below the jupon, or at the joints under the armpits. In some cases the leather jupon might have been lined with steel.

The helmet takes the form of the pointed bascinet, a light type originally worn under the great crested helm, but by the last quarter of the fourteenth century the latter had been discarded for actual warfare as too cumbrous, and was only used in tournaments. It was retained on the monuments with its distinguishing crest as a support for the head of most knights. Though a vizor was probably attached to the bascinets for fighting it seldom appears on the effigies. The bascinet of the knight at Penmynydd in Anglesey (135) is fluted.

Richly decorated sword-belts, often set with jewels, and magnificently designed clasps are very decorative features. To begin with, these are of the horizontal type, worn rather low on the hips, and are usually formed of a series of squares decorated with a conventional flower pattern, though a few of the earlier knights have round bosses, as at Meriden (157). About 1400 the sloping bawdric or sword-belt began to come into use, as in the later Swine effigies (159). In most of the richly carved figures of the first half of the fifteenth century the bawdric is used in addition to the horizontal hip-belt, though the use of the latter seems purely decorative, and its only function to support the misericorde, or dagger, on the right side. The splendid effigies at Tong and Dennington (176) may be cited as examples, though these belong to our period III. Both kinds of sword-belt are used in period IV, but it becomes less usual for both to be used together, and the hip-belt gradually disappears.

Ladies at first wear the framed or 'nebuly' head-dress of the previous period, either square or rounded and made up with a kind of honeycomb of crimped frills. Widows usually are given a simple veil over the head. In the earliest examples a tight-fitting garment with large buttons down the front is worn over the upper part of the body, above the long skirt or kirtle, but later the sleeveless *côte-hardi*, with the sides cut away under the arms, becomes more fashionable. The cloak, drawn more over the breast in later figures, is fastened by elaborate strings and brooches. In the later part of this period the framed head-dress drops out of use and more elaborate arrangements of hair-nets and veils lead on to the extravagant fashions of the next class.

Good early examples of period II may be found in Thomas Beauchamp, Earl of Warwick, d. 1371, at Warwick (148), and Thomas, Lord Berkeley, d. 1364, at Berkeley. Both of these lie on great table tombs with their wives beside them in long cloaks and framed, or nebuly, head-dresses, in these rounded, not square, and in front almost suggesting a modern lord chancellor's wig (113). In the Earl of Warwick the jupon is bulged out in a way that indicates the wearing of a steel breastplate underneath.

The knight and lady at East Harling (134, 133) are also excellent specimens of the earlier types.

The first of the De Vere effigies from Colne Priory (139) is another early figure of this class, and those at Bunbury (156) and Meriden (157) of the next stage.

The knight at Spratton has already been alluded to as the first wearer of the SS collar (143). He is an excellent specimen of the armour of the earlier part of the period, and those at Barmston (24) and Layer Marney (23) of *c*. 1400 or soon after.

The figure probably representing Sir Gervase Clifton at Clifton, near Nottingham (140), may be taken as typical of the martial effigies of the reign of Richard II. The camail is well shown, and the elaborate decorations covering the joints of the armour on arms and legs add the richness of effect which the alabaster men loved. On the jupon the lion rampant of the Cliftons is carved in low relief. Another effigy in the same church (141, 236) may be taken as his wife and is a good example of female costume of the time. She has discarded the clumsy framed head-dress worn at the middle of the century and the hair is confined in an elaborately jewelled net with a kerchief thrown over the top, and brought down lower in the middle in front. In some cases the ladies seem to have even shaved their foreheads, the notion being that this gave them a more intellectual appearance! There was considerable variety in these head-dresses towards the end of the century; Lady Marmion at Tanfield wears a close-fitting cap (154) and in other cases, as at Swine (144), a simple kerchief or veil is thrown over the head more in the fashion of the thirteenth century. In the latter case it may signify that the lady was a widow, and this was certainly so when worn with a barbe, a piece of crimped material drawn over the chin and covering the neck, as at Harewood and Lingfield (114, 116).

The knight beside the lady at Swine is an excellent example of the earlier type of camail and jupon knight, just as the later warriors in the same church (145, 159) are among our best specimens of its later development. He wears steel protection at the joints, on shoulder, elbow and knee, and the leather jupon ends in a scalloped fringe, below which the end of the mail shirt is shown. The jupon is embroidered with the chaplet of Lascelles, and he is believed to be a member of the Hilton family, one of whom had married a Lascelles heiress. The elaborate hip-belt, from which the misericorde, or dagger, once hung, is a feature in all these figures.

About 1400 there is a tendency to greater elaboration, though without any marked alteration of general type. The ridge of the bascinet, from which the camail hangs, becomes more emphasised, and the narrow bands of chased ornament over the joints, noted at Clifton, become commoner. The orle, or jewelled chaplet worn round the bascinet, described on p. 40, also becomes a usual feature, and adds greatly to the decorative effect. It began, apparently, as a flat decorative band, as in the figure of Sir Hugh Calveley, d. 1393, at Bunbury, Cheshire (156), and at Birmingham and Wootton Wawen (168) looks more like a chain, but soon became a kind of padded roll, enriched with embroidery and jewels, as in the fine effigy of William, Lord Rous, K.G., d. 1414, at Bottesford (204). This figure rests his head on a good example of the great tilting helm, or heaume, crowned with its peacock crest, and the SS collar is worn over the camail. The knight at Nuttall (142) and the later ones at Swine (145, 159) are typical specimens of this later type of the camail and jupon warriors. The joints of the armour, especially on arms and legs, are enriched with the narrow bands of ornament referred to above, which give these figures a very sumptuous appearance. Some idea of the elaboration of detail in the later examples of this period may be gained by examining the sword-hilt and scabbard of the knight at Meriden (232), a feature which has been unfortunately broken off in so many of the effigies that have come down to us.

The great tombs, surrounded by weepers, at Elford and Strelley (149, 150), rank among the finest of the later examples of our type II. That at Elford is usually attributed to Sir Thomas Arderne, d. 1391, but the well-developed orle, the

SS collar and the advanced costume of the lady suggest that it is more likely his son, Sir John, who died in 1408 and directed in his will that his body should be buried in the chancel of Elford church. Like the Earl and Countess of Warwick, husband and wife clasp one another by the hand, and the swelling breastplate is again indicated. The lady has discarded the framework of frills, and her hair is arranged in an elaborately jewelled net. Her cloak is drawn more over her shoulders, the buttons disappear, and the whole effect is richer and more graceful than that of the tight and rather ungainly costumes of Edward III's reign. This tomb was restored by Richardson, but, though perhaps more drastic in his methods than we should now approve of, he was a real sculptor and antiquary, and the work was well done. Fortunately he published a careful account in 1852 of what he did and of the condition in which he found things.

The knight was broken in two. Restorations included angel's hands and parts of arms; apex of bascinet and part of orle, the word JESU on frontal; left eye, nose, piece of cuff and left forefinger, two-thirds of handle and three-quarters of scabbard of sword; handle and end of dagger, part of lion's tail; toes, elbow-pieces, spurs; initials, dates and gashes gritted down and stopped. Of the lady he renewed one angel's head and part of face of the other, one ear and part of nose, two fingers, parts of cordon, piece of plinth and cushion and foreparts of dog; tassels of cushion, right side and back of head-dress, SS collar, fastenings and ornaments were decayed and worn, but were 'recovered', together with joined hands and nose of dog. Initials, dates, etc., were removed.

The tomb at Strelley is usually considered to be that of Sir Sampson Strelley who died about 1391, but might be a few years after that date, as his lady's head-dress is an early form of a new fashion which became common about 1415; the hair is confined in a kind of net or 'caul', projecting on each side over the ears and the two sides joined by a jewelled band over the forehead. The knight holds his gauntlet in one hand and clasps his wife's hand with the other. The camail is not carved, but there is an unsatisfactory look about the head of the knight that suggests that it may have been tampered with by a restorer. The later tombs of this class, such as those just mentioned at Bottesford, Elford and Strelley, are really of a type transitional between our classes II and III, and some of them rank with those of the next class as the masterpieces of the alabaster craftsmen. Though the new, type of all-plate armour came in about 1415, some of the more conservative-minded warriors like the Earl of Westmorland at Staindrop, d. 1425 (146), seem to have retained the camail for another ten or fifteen years instead of adopting the inflexible gorget. Among the finest of these transitional figures the splendid monument of Sir William Wilcote at Northleigh is worthy of special mention (153). Both he and his lady wear the SS collar, and Lady Wilcote wears a fur-lined cloak and a high collar which gives a distinctive look to this figure. Her hair is confined in very richly jewelled cauls, which are still of moderate size and do not project so far on each side as those of the next period. She also has a very rich chaplet. The fine tomb of Sir J. Mainwaring and his lady at Over Peover, Cheshire, is very like that at Northleigh, and is probably by the same hand (187). Lady Mainwaring's figure with its high collar and straight parallel folds of drapery is very close to that of Lady Wilcote. The same high collar and straight folds are also found in the notable effigy at Willoughby-in-the-Wolds, attributed to the Judge Sir Richard Willoughby, who died in 1362, but if this is correct the tomb must have been set up some years after his death (166).

The garment worn by these last three figures is the *houppe-lande*, a fashionable gown worn by both men and women during the first half of the fifteenth century, the only difference between the male and female dress being that the former was shorter. It has long hanging sleeves, and is arranged with straight tubular folds, usually held in at the waist by a jewelled strap or girdle. The high stiff collar was turned down and opened in front in later examples (167).

Perhaps the finest example of the last stage of our class II is the already mentioned great tomb at Staindrop of Ralph Nevill, first Earl of Westmorland, and his two wives (146). He died in 1425, and unless the monument was set up in his lifetime it must be later in date than the dated tomb at Lowick of 1419, in which the camail has been discarded, and which introduces the type of armour described in our next section.

Ecclesiastical figures of this period may be illustrated by the Bishops of Wells and Winchester. Bishop Edington, d. 1366, at Winchester (125), is a striking figure retaining much of the feeling of the earlier part of the century. The smooth drapery over the breast and varied folds lower down reveal few of the mannerisms into which the alabaster carvers fell later on. Bishop Ralph at Wells, d. 1363 (191), has suffered more from ill-treatment, but has been a fine ascetic figure, with details very richly carved, and is not far removed in general type from Archbishop Stratford at Canterbury (184) described in our section I. There is a little nearer approach to the linear draperies and sharp angular cutting with which we become familiar fifty years later. Archbishop Langham, d. 1376 (161), at Westminster[1] is another fine well-preserved figure retaining much of the free treatment of the earlier part of the fourteenth century, and the same may be said to some

---

[1] A payment to Henry Yevele for this tomb is recorded, see Lethaby, *Westminster Abbey and the King's Craftsmen*, p. 216. Yevele was Edward III's master mason, who seems to have been responsible for the nave of the abbey. He probably made the tomb, but it does not follow that he was the sculptor of the alabaster effigy on the top. Possibly, however, this may be taken as a London work.

extent of Bishop Mitford, d. 1404, at Salisbury.[1] Towards the end of the fourteenth century we find a rather heavier, coarser type, as in Bishop Harewell at Wells, d. 1386 (126). His thick bull-neck and the heavy folds of his chasuble are in strong contrast with the more refined type of Bishop Ralph. Archbishop Courtenay (d. 1396) at Canterbury, is a fine bold figure (192), but again lacks the refinement of the earlier Archbishop Stratford (184). This effigy is very like the almost contemporary one of William of Wykeham (d. 1404) at Winchester (162, 193). This last, thanks to its fine preservation,[2] enables us to form a juster idea of the gorgeous effect of these alabaster tombs than almost any other. The feet rest upon three little figures of monks whose striking features mark them out as masterpieces of early fifteenth-century work (163).

The effigy of a priest at Barrow-upon-Trent (287) is a good, though rather broken, example of one of the inferior clergy. It is difficult to date these figures, but the folds of the drapery and arrangement of the hair suggest a fourteenth-century date.

There are also some interesting civilian tombs of this period, one of the best being that supposed to be that of Sir William de la Pole (d. 1366) at Hull (132), the founder of the famous Suffolk family, and another that of John Oteswich and his wife, a London merchant, in Great St Helen's Church in the City (131). These merchants are bearded and wear a

---

[1] Murray's *Handbook to the Cathedrals of England* describes Bishop Mitford as of white marble. The tomb chest is certainly of alabaster, but the effigy is of a finer and whiter texture than the rest, though I think this too is probably of alabaster.

[2] When the Puritan soldiers were making havoc of the fittings and sculptures of the cathedral, this tomb was protected by one of their officers, Colonel Fiennes, who had been educated at Wykeham's College and maintained some respect for the founder by whose munificence he had benefited.

long gown, a short sword and a purse or wallet suspended from the belt. Oteswich has a good example of the houppelande described above (p. 54). The ladies are modestly veiled, and both these monuments retain some of the feeling of earlier fourteenth-century style. The judge at Willoughby-in-the-Wolds has already been referred to (166). His bald head, unfortunately partly repaired in plaster, gives this figure a striking and individual expression.

PERIOD III

THE LANCASTRIAN (OR EARLY PLATE), 1415–50

About the date of the battle of Agincourt the mail begins to be discarded in favour of plate armour, or at any rate to be almost entirely covered by the newer form of protection. A stiff projecting gorget is now used to cover the neck instead of the more flexible camail, though at first the camail is retained underneath with its lower end showing beneath the plate, as at Lowick (180) and Ashwellthorpe (84). Later, as at Dennington (176, 178) and Tong (181) the gorget comes directly on to the breastplate. From this time on jupons and surcoats are discarded, though the tabard, a loose short heraldic vest, occurs occasionally, as on the Earl of Somerset and Duke of Clarence at Canterbury (190). The bascinet is usually beautifully decorated, and often has the sacred name or monogram inscribed in front, as at Longford (86) and Weobley (89). The richly carved orle is almost always employed, and becomes larger and more elaborate as time goes on. In the Lowick tomb of 1420 (180) the thighs are covered with a number of small square plates apparently bolted or fixed on a leather support. This is a transitional form and was soon replaced by a system of narrow overlapping strips, or lames, of steel, known as a *fauld*. As time goes on small pendant plates, at first of rectangular shape and later of that of shields, called *tasses* or *taces*, are bolted or strapped to the lowest lame of the fauld, as at Dennington (178) or Merevale (170). The small roundels on elbow and shoulder are replaced by more scientifically shaped elbow-cops and overlapping shoulder-pieces called *pauldrons*, as at Tong (181), or Over Peover (199). *Poleyns*, or knee-cops, also become more elaborate with a kind of double wing on the outside.

The ladies wear a development of the head-dress at Strelley described above (p. 53), with the hair confined in two elaborately jewelled nets on each side over the ears, joined by a richly decorated band across the forehead and a light kerchief hanging down behind, as at Ashwellthorpe (85), or Harewood (167). This is usually known as the *crespine* head-dress from the crespine, or jewelled net, which is so prominent a feature in it. In the later examples we find the horned or mitred head-dress, in which the hair is worked up into two points on each side, like a bishop's mitre put on sideways, as at Dennington (178) or Horwood (226). Cloaks or mantles have elaborate clasps, and are joined by strings and tassels over the breast.

Among the earlier examples of this type we may single out for special mention the great double tombs of Ralph Greene[1] (d. 1419) at Lowick (180) and of Sir Edmund de Thorpe (d. 1417) at Ashwellthorpe (84, 85), both of which have been referred to above as typical of certain details. The later examples are very striking, and the great tombs of Sir Richard Vernon, d. 1451, at Tong (181) and of Lord Bardolf, K.G. (d. 1441) at Dennington (176), display perhaps the finest and most imposing of all the alabaster knights that have come down to us, and fortunately they are comparatively well preserved.

---

[1] Ralph was son of Sir Henry Greene, who figures in Shakespeare as a lord in attendance on Richard II. He was beheaded by Henry IV and his great estates confiscated, but Ralph seems to have recovered them, and they remained in the family till they passed by the marriage of the heiress, Constance Greene, to the Earl of Wiltshire, the tomb of whose son and heir is also in Lowick church.

Other notable examples may be found at Merevale (170), attributed in the guide books to an obscure bailiff of Coventry, but much more likely a Lord Ferrers; at Tideswell (169), attributed to Sir Thurstan de Bower, and at Wimborne in the monument of John Beaufort, Duke of Somerset, d. 1444 (81). Other good examples may be found at Porlock (172), East Shefford (173), Ashbourne (174), Bottesford (175) and the lady at Polesworth (155).

The knights at Merevale and Willoughby-in-the-Wolds (170, 158) are wearing what appears to be an early form of salet instead of the usual bascinet. This was a light fighting helmet brought down low over the back of the neck, something like a modern 'sou'-wester', designed to replace the cumbrous tilting helm, which could only be worn for a short while at a time, and had proved too clumsy for the varied tactics of a real battle. John Fitzalan, ninth Earl of Arundel (d. 1435), has a round topped bascinet with holes to which a vizor might have been attached in some other material: this is an exceptional figure, and wears an early example of the heraldic tabard over his armour, a feature which only becomes common at the end of the century (271).

The superb monument at Canterbury to Henry IV (d. 1413), and his queen Joan, belongs to this period and is one of the masterpieces of the alabaster men (182, 185). The jewels of the crowns, the magnificent clasps of the mantles and the richly carved borders of the royal robes are finely worked, and display the suitability of the material for elaborate detail. The queen wears the SS collar. Another notable tomb is that of Thomas, Earl of Arundel (d. 1416) and his countess (d. 1439) at Arundel (6, 138). He is represented in coronet and peer's robes instead of armour, and the countess wears the most marvellous spreading head-dress (188), some 22 in. across. The tomb of Margaret Holland (d. 1437), step-daughter of the Black Prince, with her two royal husbands

John, Earl of Somerset, and Thomas, Duke of Clarence, has also been mentioned, and here again the details of coronets and jewellery are very rich (190). Yet another semi-royal tomb of this period has come down to us. It is that of John Holland, Duke of Exeter (d. 1448), and originally stood in St Katharine's Chapel by the Tower, but was moved to the new chapel by Regent's Park when the old one was pulled down to make room for the docks. The duke is clad in a long robe and wears his coronet, and beside him lie his two wives (or, according to one record, his wife and sister). The face of one of the latter appears to have been renewed. Both the ladies are on one side instead of one on each side of their lord, as is usual, but this is possibly because this was a wall tomb and it was thought right to have the chief figure in front (171).

Interesting effigies of civilians and their wives exist at Aston-on-Trent (151) and at Harlaxton. The merchant at Aston has a curious kind of turban wound round his head, which seems to be the *chaperon* described on p. 40, and the figure at Harlaxton also has a queer-looking cap. Both their wives have the fashionable costume of the day and the bunches of hair on each side like the knights' dames.

It is interesting to find at Nottingham, the headquarters of the alabaster trade, a rather worn effigy supposed to represent John Salmon, thrice mayor of the city, who died in 1416. He wears a curious kind of tall hat with a turned-up brim (195).

The well-preserved tomb of Sir William Gascoigne at Harewood must also be mentioned here (167). This was the judge rendered famous by Shakespeare, who describes him as having dared to commit Henry V, when Prince of Wales, for unruly conduct, and who was chosen as Lord Chief Justice by that magnanimous monarch when he came to the throne as one who would be likely to administer justice without fear or favour. Our illustration shows clearly the distinctive coif worn by the judge. His robes were originally painted red, and traces of colour can still be found in some of the hollows. A priest of about this period remains at Yelvertoft (288), but the typical ecclesiastic of the period may be found in Bishop Stafford at Exeter. He was at one time Lord Chancellor of England and died in 1419. The elaborate canopy over his head recalls the Lowick gablettes of about the same date, and we may therefore have here another production of the Chellaston firm (197).

PERIOD IV

THE YORKIST (FLUTED-ARMOUR), 1440–85

It might be more correct to label this period that of the Wars of the Roses, as it begins before the middle of the century, while Edward IV did not gain his throne till 1461, but the dynastic name is conveniently short and fits in better with the titles chosen for the other periods, and many of the most characteristic figures wear the Yorkist collar of suns and roses. It is used here with the one reservation that the change of style begins to show itself ten to twenty years before the end of the reign of Henry VI. In this section we reach the complete development of what writers on armour call the 'Gothic' armour, in which the masterpieces of the medieval smith were produced.

It is a remarkable fact that before 1440 the bare-headed warrior is almost unknown, while after 1455 the helmeted knight is almost equally rare. There are two knights lying beside one another at Cheadle which are precisely similar with the exception that one wears bascinet and gorget of plate, while the other is bare-headed (200).

Henceforward heads still rest upon the great crested tilting helm, but the bascinet disappears entirely, though in three or four instances the salet, the later form of fighting helmet, is substituted. This period is also marked by a tendency to great elaboration of the accessory armour plates, such as those protecting the joints, which stand out more than they had ever done before. Coudes, or elbow-cops, especially become very large and spread out like the wings of a butterfly, and are attached by elaborately tied laces. Ridges and flutings cover the broader pieces, apparently devised with the intention of turning aside the hostile weapon and causing it to glance off harmlessly from the vital points. The tasses, or pointed plates hanging from the fauld, become larger and more important, and the gorget of plate is usually replaced by a smooth collar of mail, known as the *standard*. The hair is worn short, at first in the unbecoming fashion familiarised by the painted portraits of Henry V, where it is cut straight round the head above the ears, the back of the neck apparently being shaved,[1] as shown in the effigies at Dodford (215) and Macclesfield (201). In another figure at Macclesfield it is brushed into a kind of roll framing the face (202). This effigy, which appears to be about 1480, is an excellent example of the elaborate armour of the period. The breast-plate is divided into two sections to make movement easier, and the tasses are buckled to one of the middle lames of the fauld instead of the bottom.

Later on hair is worn slightly longer, coming down a little behind the ears as in the Fitzherberts at Norbury (206). In one of these the ends are elaborately curled (98). Henceforward all faces are clean-shaven, and remain so till well on in the reign of Henry VIII.

Ladies sometimes still continue the horned head-dress, but this soon develops into the wonderful structure known as the butterfly head-dress. The points of the horned type are straightened out and brought close together, and a trailing veil or kerchief of light thin material hangs down from them

---

[1] Sometimes referred to as the "bowl-crop".

behind. In the brasses it looks as though this were stretched over a wire frame, but in the effigies in the round there is no sign of any framework beyond that supporting the long points, and the fluttering kerchief behind is naturally less effective when the head is resting on a cushion. In later examples a broad flap is turned back round the face, from behind which the pointed structure rises, as at Marnhull (233), Kinlet (252) and St Helen's, Bishopsgate, London (242). In some instances, about 1475 to 1490, this flap is extended down over the shoulders, and a kind of truncated pyramid is substituted for the two points, as at South Cowton (115). Perhaps this is a variant of the tall steeple head-dress of the pictures and manuscripts, which has been so effective in our modern pageants, but which, as already stated, must have been a French or Burgundian fashion, as it never appears on English monuments, though in any case it could hardly have been carved on a recumbent figure. During this period the fashion of wearing the hair long and loose comes into favour, as in the thirteenth-century bronze of Queen Eleanor, which had been based, to some extent, on the contemporary representations of the Madonna. The head is usually encircled by a coronet or a kind of orle, somewhat similar to that worn by the knights of the preceding period round their bascinets. Early examples occur at Burton Agnes (221) where a veil is thrown over the top of the head, and at Thornhill (234), though in this last case it is more of a jewelled band than a regular orle. This fashion, however, is commoner in the later Tudor period, especially in the case of very great ladies entitled to wear a coronet, which was difficult to combine with the more elaborate head-dresses.

An early example of period IV may be found at Lingfield, Surrey, in the figure of Sir Reynold Cobham, who fought at Agincourt and died in 1446, leaving a will directing the burial of his body before the high altar of this church (205).

His lady, who died in 1453, is shown as a widow with a veil over her head and barbe over her chin (116), a restful and pleasing treatment after the gorgeous head-dresses of the fashionable ladies of the day. A very fine example of a widow in veil and barbe may be found at Harewood (114) where she lies beside the husband she had survived.

Another good early example of the bare-headed knight is that mentioned above at Dodford, Northants, commemorating Sir John Cressy, a distinguished soldier in the French wars, who died in 1444 (215). The same hair treatment, like a skull cap, and the elaborate accessories may be noticed. Round the tomb is the inscription in Latin giving his name and exploits quoted on p. 35.

A fine knight at Ash, Kent (216) appears to be slightly later. His forehead is represented as bald, giving the impression of a portrait. Over his armour he wears a loose heraldic tabard. The tabard becomes commoner during this period, and besides the knight at Ash, good examples occur at Harewood (222) and Methley (223). Sir John Crosby in St Helen's Church, London (242), wears a cloak over his shoulders like the Garter knights, but of course without the badges.

Among the most elaborate examples with the ridged and fluted plates we may make special mention of Robert, Lord Hungerford, at Salisbury, d. 1459 (220, 239), an almost exact counterpart of Sir J. Chideock at Christchurch, and a knight at Little Dunmow (212). The enormous elbow-pieces and elaborate laces and straps for fastening the complicated plates can be clearly seen. It is recorded that after a battle the squires and armourers held a sort of inquest over the bodies of the slain in order to discuss how best to prevent or ward off the blows that had proved fatal in the fray. The results of their conclusions, however, were not always satisfactory, as armour became so heavy that in some fights knights were found dead from exhaustion, without any sign of blows or wounds.

The superb tombs of the Fitzherberts at Norbury are a little more advanced. Sir Nicholas (206) died in 1473, and Sir Ralph (98, 213) ten years later, but both tombs are evidently by the same hand. The hair is rather longer, that of Sir Ralph being elaborately curled at the tips. The details can be well seen in the photograph of Sir Nicholas and need not be recapitulated. He wears the Yorkist collar of suns and roses, and his crest of a mailed fist is seen on the helm on which his head is resting. Other excellent specimens of this type are shown in the illustrations from Minster Lovell (219), Thornton (217), Bletchley (218) (much restored[1]), Burton Agnes (221), Harewood (222) and Methley (223). The Gascoigne knight at Harewood in the elaborately fluted armour is given an uncomfortably tight waist (207). The lady corresponding to the Thornton knight (228) and details of the ladies at Harewood (114) and South Cowton (115) may also be seen in our photographs. As stated above, two of these knights, at Harewood and Methley, wear the tabard. Lord Welles at Methley has his device of lions rampant carved in low relief on the tabard, but at Harewood it is quite smooth and must have had the arms painted upon it.

In the latest knights of this series, c. 1470–80, the hair is worn down to the shoulders, and the armour is gradually simplified. Figures of the transitional period between this class and the next are of less even workmanship, and sometimes fall below the standard usually attained by the alabaster shops, as in the two figures lying side by side at Berkeley. A late example of good workmanship remains at South Cowton, Yorks (224). It is attributed to Sir Richard Conyers, who died in 1493, and who built the neighbouring castle. It has the long hair of the Tudor period, but the elaborate armour indicates a rather earlier date, and it was probably ordered

---

[1] The hair certainly looks all wrong.

during his lifetime, probably on the death of his first wife, as there are two lady effigies of about this date preserved in the church, though not in their original position. His Tudor collar of SS and roses, however, indicates a date after 1485, so that he must have shown rather a conservative taste in the design of his ridged and fluted-armour.

Another late figure of this type at Ryther in Yorks (196, 235) illustrates the elaborate shaping and design of the armour; the standard of mail about his neck is also decorated with a series of triangular ornaments.

The last phase of the Yorkist knight may be illustrated by Sir Humphrey Blount at Kinlet, d. 1478 (252). The armour is less flamboyant and is somewhat coarse and dry in treatment, while the hair is worn a little longer. Lady Blount wears the high peaked cap with a broad flap turned back, to which attention has already been called, and which seems to be a moderate version of the butterfly head-dress of the brasses.

Four or five knights only of this period wear any form of helmet. This, as already explained, is not the bascinet, but the salet, a light fighting helmet adopted during the second half of the fifteenth century for real warfare, in place of the cumbrous tilting helm, though the latter continues to be used as a head-rest on the tombs. The salet has a long back extension to cover the back of the neck, and is sometimes fitted with a movable vizor. In some of the knights in plate gorgets, of the preceding period, the bascinet had been extended backwards to cover the back of the neck, as at Merevale (99), and at Willoughby-in-the-Wolds (88), and it may have been from this that the new salet had its origin. An early example may be found at Kidderminster in the tomb attributed to Sir Hugh Cokesay, who died in 1445. It has a raised vizor and is decorated with ridges which meet in a blunt point at the top (230). The effigy is rather worn, but the armour over which the tabard is worn must have been of a transitional type between that of our periods III and IV. Another example may be found in the rather coarse knight at Beaumaris (136) and a better one at Burghill, néar Hereford (189). The Royal Commission Volume attributes this to Sir John Milbourne, and dates it *c*. 1440, but the standard of mail and the lady's head-dress, which is almost of the butterfly pattern, suggest a slightly later date.

The other helmeted knights of this period are a little later, dating from about 1470, and are three in number. They lie close together in Dorset, one at Puddletown, and two at Melbury Sampford. All three are good examples of the elaborate Yorkist armour and wear the Yorkist collar of suns and roses. The Puddletown knight (97, 214) has a raised vizor which could be pulled down over the face. The shield beside him must be a modern mistaken restoration, as such a thing is not found on any alabaster tomb after our period I. The two figures at Melbury Sampford (231) are practically identical. Their salets have ridges rising to the point, and are decorated with round knobs, but have no vizor.[1] Their gorgets are replaced by a lighter plate protecting the front, and bent forward under the chin to form a kind of *mentonnière*, but allowing the camail worn underneath to show through at the back. These two figures are exceptionally well preserved, but all traces of colour have been removed. All three of these Dorset knights lie on Purbeck marble tombs beneath elaborate canopies of local manufacture, and it is tempting to regard their unusual features as perhaps an indication of the existence of a local school which imported the alabaster in

---

[1] An example of salet occurs in stone at Meriden, and at Brancepeth in wood. The latter belongs to the figure identified as the second Earl of Westmorland (d. 1484). Sir William St John Hope has suggested that this was the wooden pattern from which the alabaster effigy was afterwards to be made. Such patterns are mentioned in the contract for the bronze effigy of the Earl of Warwick.

block and carved the figures themselves, as had been done at London at the outset. The Purbeck marblers had long given up figure sculpture, but were doing a large trade in plain or panelled tombs, often with canopies, in the latter part of the fifteenth century. Could these Dorset knights have been an attempt to get back their old trade by importing the fashionable and easily worked material for the figures? Against this it must be confessed that they are accomplished works and certainly do not look like experiments. Possibly there was a skilful establishment of tomb makers at Bristol, or some other big western town, which provided such figures, and the helmeted figures were a concession to the conservative taste of the provincial nobility.

The rather small ladies, about 4 ft. long, at Stourton Caundle, Horwood and Ilton (227, 226, 229) present certain unusual features, such as the children carved in miniature in the draperies at the sides of the first two, and these too suggest the existence of a special workshop supplying figures to the west country. Could this also have been Bristol? Too much must not be made of the children at the side as they occur elsewhere in widely different types of monument. We have already mentioned the chrism child at Kinlet (225) and the small versions of the big effigies placed on either side of the tomb at Burton Agnes, Yorks (221), but the treatment here is quite unlike that of the Devon and Dorset examples, where the children are arranged one above another in a sort of column in the folds of their mother's cloak.

Ecclesiastics may be represented by Abbot Seabroke at Gloucester, d. 1457 (127), to whom reference was made earlier in this paper, when it was pointed out that the style of these figures did not alter very much as one period succeeded another. The rather dry linear treatment of the drapery is perhaps most characteristic of the period of which we are treating.

One of the most sumptuous monuments of this period is that of Bishop Beckyngton at Wells. He died in 1465, but it is recorded that he dedicated the altar in his own chantry chapel thirteen years earlier in 1452, and thus lived with this *memento mori* before his eyes all that time. The chantry chapel was taken to pieces in 1850, but has now fortunately been restored. The effigy only is of alabaster, and is much worn. The face is wrinkled and aged, and as the bishop ordered it himself it may be more of a portrait than is usually the case. The details are very carefully wrought (194). Under the tomb is a cadaver in stone.[1]

We have no royal effigies of this date, but the most splendid tomb of a semi-royal kind is that of Alice, Duchess of Suffolk, d. 1477, at Ewelme (183). She was widow of the unfortunate William de la Pole, Duke of Suffolk, who was murdered at sea in 1450, and she is represented with coronet worn over her widow's veil.

A curious and interesting variety on the stock figures is that of a man of Lutterworth with a long gown worn over his armour. It is difficult to say what precisely this is meant to indicate. A much decayed figure, supposed to represent the judge, Sir William Portington (d. 1462), at Eastrington near Howden, wears the judge's close-fitting coif and robes over armour, which appears on his right side. This figure is unfortunately in very poor preservation.

In assigning tombs of this section to particular groups we have already mentioned that Lord Hungerford at Salisbury (220) is practically a duplicate of Sir J. Chideock at Christchurch. The broken figure of Sir Thomas Greene at Greene's Norton might perhaps be added to the group. Among later examples the knight at Ryther, Yorks (196) and a sadly defaced one at Puddletown, Dorset, are extraordinarily similar

---

[1] See Dr Fryer, F.S.A. in *Proceedings of Somersetshire Archaeological and Nat. Hist. Society*, 1923.

in detail and in pose with the head rather thrown back. The canopies of the weepers are of a very similar type though those at Ryther are relations (56) and those at Puddletown angels. The pose of Sir Robert Harcourt at Stanton Harcourt is also very much like these effigies, though variety is given by his Garter robes, and his tomb chest is ornamented merely by shields and panelling (177).

PERIOD V

THE EARLY TUDOR, 1485–1540

The fifth class is that of the Tudor period, and lasts from the accession of Henry VII after the battle of Bosworth in 1485, to the end of the Gothic inspiration in Henry VIII's reign. It is perhaps better to call it the Early Tudor period, as students of armour who continue their researches through the Renaissance period would probably use the term 'Tudor' for the highly embossed and gorgeous, though less graceful, suits of armour of the Elizabethan age. The break between the fourth and fifth periods is less clearly marked than that between the third and fourth. The chief difference between the later and the earlier is seen in greater restraint and some simplification of the armour. The fantastic projections are reduced, and smoother plates without the ridges and flutings come into use, as being more suitable for actual warfare than for the tournament. The pauldrons, or shoulder-pieces, are no longer a set of overlapping plates, but are usually formed of a large smooth plate with a bold projection at the top to stop a blow aimed at the neck. This is often much larger on the left side as more exposed to the thrust of a lance.

When the early years of the sixteenth century are reached, the pointed shoes of overlapping plates, known as sollerets, or sabatons, are superseded by blunt and square-toed foot coverings which are more practical, if less ornamental (109,

110). The overlapping lames of the fauld are reduced in number, and the tasses become much larger and are bolted or strapped to the upper lames instead of the lower. A kind of skirt of mail usually shows under them which by this time may only be suspended from the waist instead of being the bottom of the complete haubergeon.

In these late tombs the mantling suspended from the helm is spread over the tomb slab in a very effective manner and the gauntlets, instead of being worn, are placed on the slab beside the figure.

Hair is worn longer and comes down to the neck or even to the shoulder. Round about 1500 it is often carefully curled, as at Harewood (243), Easebourne (272), Salisbury (266) or Clifton (245). By the beginning of the reign of Henry VIII it is frequently cut straight across the forehead, rather like the 'bobbed' hair of so many little girls of to-day, if we may use a slang term. In many cases it is represented in a very summary way by a series of parallel ridges, as at Ratcliffe-on-Soar (247) or the Daubeny monument at Westminster (280), but this rather harsh treatment may have been partly modified by the painting which has now usually perished.

Ladies' dress varies very little throughout the fifteenth century, except in the head-dress. In the earlier examples of this period the cap with broad flap turned back is the commonest, but about the year 1500 a rigid framework is inserted coming to a point in the middle, giving the cap something the shape of a low gable. This is known as the *pedimental* head-dress. At first the veil on each side falls low on the shoulders, as shown at Chipping Norton (253), Prestwold (263) or Godshill (238), but later the side pieces are stiffened and cut off short, as may be seen at Middle Claydon and Duffield (264, 265). These stiff frames were usually embroidered or covered with lace, as at Fawsley (274).

Right at the end of our period, as the first signs of the approaching Renaissance and Italian influences begin to appear, we find what is known as a Paris, or French cap, made familiar by pictures of Mary Queen of Scots, and this is usually accompanied by padded sleeves, something in the manner of those of a modern bishop. What is meant by this description can best be seen by reference to the ladies at Eye and Stanford-on-Avon (254, 305) in our photographs. The husband of the former wears a fine example of the tabard, which occurs again and again at various dates throughout the century.

Very great ladies sometimes wear their hair loose, falling down over their shoulders, and crowned with a coronet. Thus, the Lady Isabella Smythe, daughter of John Nevill, Marquess of Montacute, brother of Warwick the Kingmaker, is represented in this manner, while Sir William Smythe's first wife, the Lady Anne Staunton, is wearing the ordinary pedimental head-dress (256, 179). Princess Elizabeth Plantagenet, Duchess of Suffolk, wears her coronet over a simple widow's veil (275), and Lady Elizabeth Ferrers at Lockington (268) is a very pleasing example. The long loose hair fashion, which in earlier days had been usually reserved for unmarried girls or queens, was also copied sometimes by dames of less exalted rank, in which case, as already mentioned, a kind of ornamental roll or chaplet, something like the knight's orle, replaces the coronet, as at Batley (261), Thurlaston (260) or Clifton, Beds (245). Widows still wore veil and barbe. At Deene the judge Sir Robert Brudenell (d. 1531) lies between his two wives. The one who predeceased him has the pedimental head-dress, while the survivor wears the widow's weeds (301).

The earlier of the two knights at Eye, Herefordshire, is an excellent example of Tudor armour (255) and shows most of the characteristics described above, while the later one in a tabard (254) is a fine specimen of the very end of the Gothic period. The beautiful and wonderfully preserved figure of Sir Henry Pierrepont at Holme Pierrepont, d. 1499 (246, 257), is also a first-rate example. He left instructions in his will, proved at York, 18 December 1499, that he 'should be buried in the church among his worshipful ancestors, and a tomb of alabaster to be made and sett upon his sepulchre, and graven by the discretion of his executors'. The tomb upon which he rests with its small shields set in lozenge-shaped panels is practically a duplicate of those of John Strelley at Strelley, d. 1501 (270), and Ralph Sacheverell, at Ratcliffe-on-Soar, d. 1539 (247), suggesting that all these tombs came from the same workshop, probably in Nottingham.[1] Other good examples of the period may be found at Chipping Norton, where a long-haired knight is lying beside his lady who wears the simple and early form of the pedimental head-dress mentioned above (253), and at Radbourne, Derbyshire, where the lady has the flapped cap (258). The great tomb of Sir William Smythe, d. 1525, with his two wives, at Elford, has been referred to again and again. His face and certain details were restored by Richardson, and the figure of his first wife Anne Staunton, through whom he inherited the Elford property, was much renewed, but the whole gives a good notion of the general effect of these later alabaster monuments in everything except the colour (256). The elaborate tomb chest with its vaulted niches and fancy traceries is very like that of Richard Vernon, Esq. (d. 1517) at Tong, and both must have a common origin (26, 25). Two fine tombs of the Mathew family at Llandaff (299) are excellent examples of the early years of Henry VIII.

The figure of Sir John Cheyney, d. 1509, at Salisbury, is a notable specimen of early sixteenth-century type. He was

---

[1] See *Arms, Armour, and Alabaster, round Nottingham*, by George Fellows, 1907.

Henry VII's standard-bearer at the battle of Bosworth, and is represented in Garter robes. His long hair and heavy jaw, combined with the smoother more business-like type of armour, give him a rather grim appearance (266). This lantern-jawed type of face reappears in a knight at Macclesfield (273) and in one of the Llandaff tombs.

The tomb at Duffield illustrates the final phase of Gothic plate-armour (265). Elbow-cops are no longer fluted and projecting, and are bolted on, not laced. The pauldrons are smooth and curve upwards at the top to provide a neck-guard. The lames of the fauld are very narrow and unimportant, while the tasses are long and heavy. The lady has the short pedimental head-dress, and padded sleeves. A still later, transitional type, may be illustrated by the tomb of Lady Margaret Gyffard, d. 1539, at Middle Claydon (264). Here the same features occur, but there is more of the Renaissance feeling, shown chiefly in the more natural and studied folds of the drapery.

One of the finest and best preserved of the alabaster tombs is that of Sir Richard Knightley and his wife at Fawsley, Northants (274). He died in 1534 and we have already had occasion to describe the remarkable series of weepers. He has the 'bobbed' hair of the period and wears an elaborately carved heraldic tabard and the Tudor form of the SS collar. His lady has the short pediment head-dress and the padded sleeves which are the first sign of the coming Renaissance. A considerable amount of colour remains, and this tomb gives as good an idea as any of the original splendour of these latest alabaster monuments.

Sir George Forster (d. 1539) at Aldermaston is of a heavier type and rather different feeling than some of those mentioned above. The twisted columns at the corners of his tomb are the heralds of the Renaissance, and occur elsewhere in Purbeck marble, as at Turvey. Possibly we have here a production of the London workshops. His lady has the later fully developed form of the pedimental head-dress, framing her face in a four-sided cap instead of falling down in a long veil over her shoulders (276). Sir George wears good examples of the square-toed sabatons. All the details of this tomb are good; the padding inside the great helm on which his head rests should be noticed (278), and the varied attitudes of the rather foppish weepers, like the padded sleeves of the lady, betray the first signs of the coming change to Renaissance types (277).

Two other monuments may be grouped with this, the Manners tomb at Windsor (279, 281) and that of Sir Giles Daubeny at Westminster (280). The former has enormous neck-guards, and the latter is distinguished by the Garter robes.

Perhaps as good a notion as any of the earlier type, c. 1490, and the latest, c. 1530, may be gained by comparing the fine examples at Harewood and Ratcliffe-on-Soar (243, 247). Already in the earlier knight we find the smooth armour without the flutings and excrescences of the Yorkist type, and the pauldrons curve upwards to form a neck-guard. The hair is long and carefully curled, and the Tudor collar of S and rose alternating is worn. His wife is represented as a widow with almost the same veil and barbe as an earlier lady at Harewood, belonging to our class IV (114), but the folds of the thin draperies are treated with greater variety and naturalism. The knight's feet rest upon a lion, and seated on the lion's back against the sole of the foot is a little bedesman (107), very like an earlier example at Norbury. The tail of the lion is twisted up and given an elaborate bunch of hair to support the other foot (see p. 37). The knight at Ratcliffe is accoutred in a very similar manner, but the pauldrons and tasses are larger, and the fauld and standard-of-mail collar are reduced in importance. The SS collar is of the later fashion with large letters and hanging lower in front. The hair is cut straight in front and behind in the 'bobbed' manner referred to above. His lady has the pedimental head-dress, and some of the slashes and bows begin to appear down the front of her dress, which become such a feature in the costume of the two ladies placed side by side on a single tomb at Prestwold (263). These have the earlier form of pedimental head-dress with long pieces hanging down on each side, which may be compared with the latest type as worn by the lady at Castle Donington (262), who also wears the padded sleeves of the latest fashion before the introduction of the Elizabethan ruffs which mark the end of the period under review.

Two or three other effigies of this period deserve mention. That attributed to Sir David Owen (d. 1542) at Easebourne (272) has the long curled hair and Tudor collar of SS and roses which are illustrated from Harewood (243). He wears the tabard. He died at the advanced age of 83, and there seems to be some evidence in his will that this effigy had been prepared some forty years before his death, which is confirmed by the style of the figure.

A very unusual figure in a tabard and long hair occurs at Apethorpe in Northamptonshire. Though the whole slab is 5 ft. 9½ in. long, the knight is only 3 ft. 9½ in., and a kind of canopy is formed by a group of the Coronation of the Virgin (79).

The long hair, carefully curled at the ends, found on the knight at Clifton, Beds (245), may be compared with the long twisted strands given to the Earl of Wiltshire at Lowick (209), who also has an elaborate tabard with his arms carved in relief. A pleasing example of the later 'bobbed-hair' type in smoother armour and with the drooping SS collar may be found at Little Chart, Kent (203).

So many of the old fighting nobility had perished in the Wars of the Roses that it is not surprising to find monuments of civilians more prominent in this last period. An excellent example may be found at Ashover, Derbyshire, attributed to Thomas Babyngton, who died in 1518. Much of the colouring remains—apparently very much refreshed—and the effect is very striking (259). The long gowns are red, the hair black, the lady's head-dress black and green, and the hands and faces are left in the natural colour of the polished alabaster. The long gown with purse or scrip hanging from the belt is exactly the costume worn by the courtiers attending the king in the famous Warwick manuscript in the British Museum.[1] There is a tomb of similar date and type to William Blythe at Norton near Sheffield. It was erected and a chantry founded by his son, Bishop Blythe of Lichfield (1503–30). An interesting civilian in long gown with scrip, or seal-bag, hanging from his belt may be found in the remote church of Chilton, Suffolk (269). A man in a long gown lies beside a lady in the short pedimental head-dress at Newport, Salop (300), and the judge in his robes and coif at Deene (301) has already been referred to. Judge William Rudhall, d. 1529, at Ross in cap and robes of office may also be mentioned (295).

As Henry VI's tomb was never completed, and Henry VII was commemorated by the imported Italian Torrigiani, we have no royal alabasters of this period, but the semi-royal tomb of the Duke of Suffolk and his duchess, Elizabeth Plantagenet, has been already mentioned (275). The duke died in 1491. He wears Garter robes and coronet, and his furrowed face and curled hair give more the effect of a portrait than is usually to be found. The great crest of a Saracen's head, on the helm on which his head rests, is a very effective work of art (108).

A remarkable effigy of this period remains at Ashby-de-la-

---

[1] *Pageant of the Birth, Life and Death of Richard Beauchamp, Earl of Warwick, K.G. 1389–1439.* Reproduced in facsimile by Viscount Dillon and Sir W. H. St John Hope, 1914.

Zouch, representing a pilgrim with palmer's staff and cloak and his head resting on a broad-brimmed hat in which is set the cockle shell of St James of Compostela. It is not known who is here commemorated, but he must have been a man of some position and importance, as he wears the SS collar (210). Another very unusual figure occurs in a late monument, c. 1540, at Coventry to Elizabeth Swillington (286) and her two husbands. The first of the two, Thomas Essex, is represented in the ordinary late Tudor armour, bare headed but with a beard, a fashion that had been in abeyance for a hundred years, though shortly to be revived by Henry VIII. This early form of beard is more like those found in the alabaster tables than the sharply pointed beard of the Elizabethan courtier. The second husband, Ralph Swillington, Recorder of Coventry and Attorney General, is in the costume of a civilian in long robe, like that at Ashover (259).

Another unusual effigy may be found at Allerton Mauleverer, Yorks, identified by Mr I'Anson, F.S.A. as Sir John Mauleverer, who died in 1458. He wears a mentonnière or beavor over his chin, and apparently had a bare head and long hair, though the monument is so terribly decayed that it is difficult to make out what it was like. The lady beside him seems to have had the flapped head-dress of c. 1490, and as far as can be judged in its present condition the monument is thirty or forty years later than the accepted date. A still more remarkable, and less mutilated figure at Bromham, Wilts (284) enables us to form some notion of what the Yorkshire knight was like. Though the surface is badly disfigured by initials this effigy is otherwise fairly well preserved. A mentonnière or beavor protects the chin, and the hair is worn long, while a round cap, turned up at the back, covers the head, quite unlike anything found elsewhere. The head is supported on cushions instead of the usual great helm. The guide books identify this tomb as that of Sir Roger Tocotes, who died in 1457, but the Purbeck marble tomb chest, and the heavy pauldrons, that on the left being bent up to form a huge neck-protector, point to a date at the end of the century. The long stern type of face and long hair also belong to a later date. This tomb is placed in the centre of a very rich late Perpendicular chapel, stated to have been built by Richard Beauchamp, Baron St Amand, who died in 1508, and it therefore seems natural to suggest that it is he who is commemorated by our effigy. It is very likely that he built the chapel some years before his death, and he would probably have ordered the tomb at the same time. His feet rest on a unicorn which appears outside the chapel as a supporter of the arms carved over the eastern gable.

The interesting figure attributed to John Noble, Principal of Broadgates Hall,[1] is preserved in St Aldate's Church, Oxford. He died in 1522, and wears what appears to be a university hood thrown over his shoulders in quite the modern manner (294).

Good examples of late ecclesiastics may be found in the boldly carved Abbot Parker (290) at Gloucester, and in the almost suspiciously well-preserved and thickly painted Bishop Penny of Carlisle at Leicester (289). The latter died in 1520, and was buried at Leicester, of which place he had previously been abbot. The naturalistic treatment of the crumpled folds of his chasuble is one of the first signs of the approaching change, and a herald of the Renaissance so soon to overwhelm our native art and replace it with Flemish and Italian ideas. Bishop Shirburne of Chichester (d. 1536) is a typical early sixteenth-century ecclesiastic (198). The colour and gilding, though no doubt refreshed in modern times, serve to bring home to us the sumptuous effect of these alabaster monuments in their original state. For a lesser dignitary,

---

[1] The old name of what afterwards became Pembroke College.

John Bothe, Treasurer of Lichfield, at Sawley is an excellent specimen (128). He died in 1496, and is habited in quire vestments instead of the more usual chasuble worn for the Mass. Another is the big priest at Birmingham, also in quire habit.

The priest at Halsall, Lancs (296) wears the furred tippet, or *amice*, with strips or tails hanging from it, and from the treatment of the hair must probably be dated *c.* 1470–80. Another ecclesiastic of *c.* 1500 is attributed to Dean Harvey (297) of Hereford.

The striking effigy of a priest in St Mary Redcliffe, Bristol, attributed to William Canynge (d. *c.* 1474) has already been referred to as exhibiting an individuality of feature almost suggesting a portrait (291). He rebuilt the church, and is said according to local tradition, which is not always trustworthy, to have two effigies, one representing him as mayor and this one as Dean of the College, in which he appears in quire habit.

In the effigy attributed to Sir Richard Newton, a judge, at Yatton (292), not far away, a strong family likeness may be detected to our Bristol figure. The rather stiff angular folds of the draperies in both effigies certainly suggest a common origin. Sir Richard died in 1449, and if the tomb is rightly attributed to him it cannot have been erected till the death of his wife in 1475. We have noted more than once certain peculiarities in these south-western effigies, which mark them off from the usual types of the Nottingham workshops, and these last two seem again to point to Bristol as the place of origin. The figure of a lay bursar of the abbey, now in the parish church at Glastonbury (211), might also be a product of this school.

PERIOD VI

POST-REFORMATION—THE GOTHIC OVERLAP

In compiling our lists we have drawn the line at the Reformation, taking the suppression of the monasteries 1536–40 as marking the end of medieval England. The introduction of Renaissance forms from Italy, either directly by such men as Torrigiani at Westminster, or still more by nameless craftsmen from Flanders or northern France, also marks the end of the Gothic tradition, but the new ideas filtered in gradually, and we cannot fix a definite date of separation between the old and the new. We English are a conservative race, and we find the alabastermen of Burton continuing to produce tombs in the middle of the sixteenth century in which the old Gothic traditions survive in spite of classical details on the tomb chests, and slight modifications of fashion in the costume of the ladies or the provision of beards for their husbands. It has, therefore, been thought well to add a sixth period to the lists, but this should be regarded as an appendix to the rest as it includes only a selection of a few typical examples of the later work in which the Gothic feeling is more evident. No attempt has been made to provide a comprehensive list, as in the previous periods, and the monuments inserted are merely there as samples. The subject has been ably dealt with by Mr J. G. Mann, F.S.A. in the Walpole Society's Twenty-first Volume 1932–3.

The old traditions lasted longer in the Midlands than elsewhere and such effigies as those of John Digby (d. 1558) at Coleshill or Sir William Fielding (d. 1547) at Monks' Kirby might easily pass for works of fifty years earlier if it were not for the French caps of the Mary Queen of Scots type worn by their ladies, and the ruffs at the wrists and pointed beard of the Digby knight. The same may be said of the fine knight in a tabard at Eye, Herefordshire (254) attributed to Sir

George Cornwall, who did not die till 1563, though this monument was probably erected in his lifetime.

The fine tomb of Sir John Vernon at Clifton Campville (68) belongs to a group with bedesmen and other weepers under broad rather clumsily foiled arcades and twisted columns at the corners, which we must probably assign to the Burton shops. Sir John did not die till 1545, but the amusing frieze of little animals and birds running round the broad moulding of the base is the only feature to distinguish it from the tomb of Robert Hazelrig (d. 1536) at Castle Donington (262), while the civilian tomb at Newport, Salop, and those of Sir R. Mynors (d. 1536) at Duffield, of Judge Rudhall at Ross (52, 63, 295), and the latest of the Savage group at Macclesfield (d. 1528), are obviously from the same source. In all these the armour is of the type that had been in use for the last twenty or thirty years, the ladies wear the short pedimental head-dress and the only late feature is the padded sleeve sometimes ending in an elementary ruff at the wrist. The costume is in both knight and lady almost exactly that of the tomb of Sir George Manners, Lord Ross (d. 1513) at Windsor (279, 281), which suggests that this last may not have been put up till his wife's death in 1526.

Even tombs erected after the middle of the century retain the general design of the older tradition. Tomb chests may have Classical pilasters to separate the weepers, and certain saints or groups could only have been allowed in Queen Mary's reign (1553–8), but the armour of the knights shows little change though beards become more common. Ladies' dresses are slashed and elaborated and puffed sleeves at the shoulders begin to anticipate the extravagant fashions of Elizabeth's reign, but the prodigious ruffs of the next period have not yet appeared. The French, or Paris cap, coming to a point against the cheek, which we associate with Mary Queen of Scots, gradually replaces the pedimental head-dress. Good examples of this type may be found in the monuments of Sir Thomas Cave (d. 1558) at Stanford-on-Avon (305) and Sir Robert Scargill (d. 1531) at Whitkirk, the latter being evidently ordered some years after his death, probably on that of his wife.

Apart from their beards, Sir Alexander Denton (d. 1566) at Hereford, and knights at Swepstone, Breedon-on-the-Hill, Faringdon and Wheathampstead show very little change in armour or accoutrements, while much Gothic tradition survives in the fine figure of Lord Chief Justice Bromley (d. 1555) at Wroxeter (303), although the tomb chest is quite Renaissance in character. The charming little figure of his daughter holding à flower, and the pheasant at his head, are signs of a search for new ideas. Even the sumptuous monument of the Earl of Huntingdon (d. 1561) at Ashby-de-la-Zouch (302) in coronet and Garter robes, with his countess in widow's barbe, is in general form quite of the old tradition.

The magnificent tomb of Thomas, first Earl of Rutland (d. 1543) at Bottesford, also in Garter robes, while conforming in general outline to the traditional form, begins to show a more realistic touch in the faces, which suggest a real attempt at portraiture. This was made by a Richard Parker, who has been identified as an alabaster worker of Burton. This tomb shows the high quality attained when the new technical skill developed abroad gave fresh inspiration, but before the clumsy semi-classical affectations of the later Renaissance vulgarised the taste of art-workers in this country. The beginning of this decline is seen in the work of the Royley firm at Burton, of whom we have records in the last quarter of the sixteenth century. The contract exists for their undertaking of the tomb of John Shirley at Breedon-on-the-Hill (1585), and two or three other monuments display so much likeness to this that they also can be attributed to Richard and Gabriel Royley, but with this class of work we are getting well beyond the limits set down for treatment in this book.

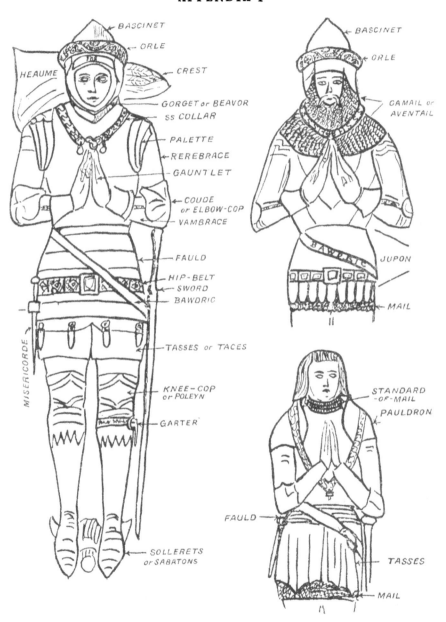

BASCINET
ORLE
HEAUME
CREST
GORGET or BEAVOR
ss COLLAR
PALETTE
REREBRACE
GAUNTLET
COUDE or ELBOW-COP
VAMBRACE
FAULD
HIP-BELT
SWORD
BAWDRIC
MISERICORDE
TASSES or TACES
KNEE-COP or POLEYN
GARTER
SOLLERETS or SABATONS

BASCINET
ORLE
CAMAIL or AVENTAIL
JUPON
MAIL

STANDARD -OF-MAIL
PAULDRON
FAULD
TASSES
MAIL

DIAGRAM OF ARMOUR
giving names of principal pieces referred to in the text

APPENDIX II

LIST OF ALABASTER EFFIGIES

The following list attempts to be almost complete in the case of the first five categories. The sixth contains a few representative examples only. They are arranged under counties, and the alphabetical list of illustrations will enable most of them to be traced. The various categories have been described in detail in Chapter IV, and as the armour and costume is fairly uniform in each class it is unnecessary to give a minute description in each individual case, special features or peculiarities being added in the column set apart for that purpose.

The names of those represented cannot always be guaranteed where no inscriptions have survived, but where names attributed by local antiquaries with the help of heraldry or local records agree with the dates suggested by the style of the armour, etc., there is usually some probability that such attributions are correct.

The following explanations and abbreviations are used:

Column 1   gives the county in which examples occur.

      2   gives the classification or type, as explained in the foregoing article, and will save a more detailed description.

      3   gives the place. In the case of cathedral towns the cathedral is meant if no other church is named.

      4   gives the description, i.e. the kind of person represented. K=knight, L=lady, C=civilian, Bp.=bishop, Abp.=archbishop, P=priest. Where two or more letters are put together, e.g. K and L, the effigies are placed side by side on the same tomb.

      5   gives the usual attribution and date.

6 indicates the present state of preservation. Slight repairs, such as new noses, and the cutting of initials, unless very bad, have been ignored.

7 gives particulars of the tomb chest, weepers, etc.

8 indicates any special features. SS = the famous Lancastrian collar of esses, and Y = the Yorkist collar of suns and roses. O = orle.

9 gives a reference to the illustrations.

County	Class	Place	Description	Usual attribution (not guaranteed)	State of preservation	Tomb chest	Special features	Illustration
Bedford	V	Clifton	K, L	Called Sir Michael Fysher, d. 1549 (looks 20 or 30 years earlier)	Good	Angels with shields. Has been moved and weepers of side against wall placed above tomb	K: hair curled over shoulders; heavy pauldrons L: long hair loose and a kind of orle	244, 245
Berkshire		Turvey	K, L	Sir John Mordaunt, d. 1504; fought at Barnet and Bosworth	Good	Purbeck with twisted columns at corners	K: wears mantle; SS L: long hair and kind of orle. Holes for fixing brass inscription	
	II	Wantage	K, L	Sir William Fitzwarren, d. 1361	Much worn	—	K: cross-legged L: frilled cap	129
	III	East Shefford	K, L	Sir Thomas Fettiplace, c. 1440	Fairly good; L's arms gone	Angels with shields	K: O	173
	V	Windsor	K, L	Sir George Manners, d. 1513	Very good	Weepers and angels; good examples of costume	K: horned head-dress K: SS; big neck-guard; feet on Unicorn L: short pediment and padded sleeves. Inscription	40, 59, 279, 281
		Windsor	K, L	Chas. Somerset, Earl of Worcester, d. 1526 and wife, d. 1506	Fairly good; faces worn	Bronze screen of Flemish workmanship	K: Garter robes; bedesmen at feet L: loose hair and band	
		Aldermaston	K, L	Sir George Forster, d. 1539 Lady Elizabeth Forster, d. 1526	Good	Weepers in varied attitudes holding small heraldic shields	K: unusual form of SS collar; note cloth lining to tilting helm L: pedimental head-dress (short). Inscription	41, 57, 276, 277, 278
	VI	Lambourne	K, L	Sir Thos. Essex, d. 1558	Good	Groups of children kneeling at end	K: tabard; small ruff and chains L: Queen of Scots cap and puffed sleeves	
Buckingham	II	Faringdon	K, L	c. 1553	—	—		
		Aylesbury	K	c. 1380	Rather worn	—		
	IV	Bletchley	L	Lord Grey of Wilton, c. 1450	Good	Weepers and angels	Breastplate indicated under jupon Widow's barbe and veil SS. Inscription	43, 152 218
		Thornton	K	(?)	Restored and spoilt			
		Thornton	L	—	Good		Collar of twisted rope	217
	VI	Middle Claydon	L	Margaret Gyffard, d. 1539	Good	Renaissance detail	Flapped head-dress Pedimental head-dress; puffed sleeves. Inscription	228 264
Cheshire	II	Bunbury	K	Sir Hugh Calveley, d. 1393. (Famous commander in French Wars—see Froissart)	Fairly good	Empty niches for weepers surrounded by original iron grate	Richly carved band round bascinet; calf badges on jupon in relief	156
		Acton	K	Sir Wm. Mainwaring, d. 1399	Fair, but much cut about with initials, etc.	—	SS; O; sacred name on bascinet; ass-head crest on helm. Inscription	
		Barthomley	K	Sir Robert Foulshurst, d. 1389	Fairly good	Tomb chest with angels later and does not belong	SS; O	64
		Over Peover	K, L	Sir John Mainwaring, d. 1410	Good	—	K: SS; O; sacred name on bascinet; ass-head crest; jupon appears to be steel-lined L: SS; high collar; small crespine head-dress	187

	County	Place		Identity	Condition	Accessories	Notes	Page
III		Over Peover	K, L	Sir Randle Mainwaring, d. 1456	Fairly good; decayed crack in L's face	—	K: SS; O; sacred name on bascinet; ass-head crest on helm; L: horned head-dress	199
IV		Cheadle	K	Sir John Hondford, d. 1461	Fair	—	SS; O	200
		Cheadle	K	Sir John Hondford, d. 1473	Fair	—	SS; except for bare head this figure is almost a duplicate of the above	200
		Macclesfield	K	Sir John Savage, d. 1463 (?)	Good	—	SS	201
		Macclesfield	K	Downes of Shrigley, c. 1470–80	Good	—	Hair in a roll; good example of elaborate type of armour	202
V		Macclesfield	K, L	Sir John Savage, d. 1495	Good	Kneeling weepers with shields	K: Y; L: collar with roses only; butterfly head-dress; hands clasped	66
		Macclesfield	K, L	Sir John Savage, d. 1513 (?)	Good	—	Chain collar; long hair	273
		Macclesfield	K, L	Sir John Savage, d. 1528 (?)	Fair	Angels and weepers	K: SS; L: pedimental head-dress (short); padded sleeves	
		Malpas	K, L	Sir Rundle Brereton, d. 1522	Restored and scraped	Angels, weepers and bedesmen. Inscription	K: SS; L: pedimental head-dress (long)	
		Barthomley	P	Robert Foulshurst, rector, d. 1529	Fairly good	—	—	
V	Cornwall	Callington	K	Lord Willoughby de Broke, K.G., d. 1503	Fair except for initials, etc.; face rubbed	Shields of arms enclosed in Garter collar	Garter robes (with badge on shoulders) and collar; bedesmen on lion at feet	83
II	Cumberland	Greystoke	K	William the Good Baron of Greystoke, d. 1367 (?)	Much worn	Canopy at head decorated with shields	—	137
IV		Greystoke	K	John, Baron Greystoke (will of 1436 directing burial in Collegiate Church of Greystoke)	Fair, but legs below knees gone	Angels and Saints (no longer in position but set up separately in wall)	SS; a circlet of flames round helm under head	
V		Millom	K, L	Sir John Hudleston, d. 1494	Much worn and legs broken	Angels with shields and little kneeling weepers beside them	K: Y; L: flapped head-dress	71
		Wetheral	K, L	Sir Richard Salkeld, c. 1500, d. 1518; probably made during lifetime	K: poor; L: much worn	—	? SS (too worn to be certain); L: flapped head-dress	
II	Derby	Bakewell	K, L	Sir Godfrey Foljambe, d. 1376	Good	—	Half effigies in frame on wall	3
		Bakewell	K	Sir Thos. Wendesley, d. 1403	Rather worn and cut with initials	—	SS; O; angels and cushions	287
III		Barrow-on-Trent	P	c. 1440	Broken and worn	—	Bare head; chasuble	
		Longford	K	—	Fair	—	Cushions only	
		Newton Solney	K	—	Fair	—	Cushion and angels	
		Tideswell	K, L	—	Fair; K's legs and L's arms broken	Two angels supporting shields on side of tomb; modern inscription	K: SS; O	169
		Ashbourne	K, L	Sir J. Cockayne, d. 1447	Fair	Panelling; angels holding shields	K: SS; O; L: horned (or heart-shaped) head-dress	22, 45, 174
		Gt. Cubley	K	—	Poor	—	SS; O	
		Longford	K	—	Fairly good	—	SS; O; I.H.S. on bascinet	86
		Aston-on-Trent	C, L	—	Fairly good	Angels holding shields; those at end kneeling	C wears a kind of turban or chaperon and houppelande; hands clasped together; L: crespine	151

County	Class	Place	Description	Usual attribution (not guaranteed)	State of preservation	Tomb chest	Special features	Illustration
Derby	IV	Ashbourne	K, L	—	Fair but patched and cracked in places	Angels holding shields	—	35, 39, 46, 206
		Repton	K	—	Rather worn	—	Y	
		Norbury	K	Nicholas Fitzherbert, 10th Lord Norbury, d. 1473	Good	Fine set of weepers; two wives at end	Y: good example of very elaborate armour; crest mailed fist on helm	10, 44, 98, 237
		Norbury	K, L	Ralph Fitzherbert, 11th Lord Norbury, d. 1483	Good	Fine set of weepers; good costumes; angels	K: Y and armour; L: butterfly; elaborate costumes; K: tips of hair curled; bedesmen on lion at feet; crest mailed fist on helm; Y	
	v	Kedleston	K	a Curzon	Fair	—	SS	78
		Youlgreave	K	Thomas Cockayne, d. 1488	Restored	—	Y: tomb and effigy about half usual size; long hair	76
		Dronfield	K, L	—	Moderate	Angels holding shields	K: SS	
		Radbourne	K, L	John Pole, c. 1500	Fairly good	Angels holding shields	L: flapped or truncated-cone head-dress	258
		Kedleston	K, L	Sir John Curzon, c. 1490	Fairly good	Angel; bedesmen and children (looks later than effigies)	K: SS; L: flapped or truncated cone	
		Norton	C, L	William Blythe, c. 1510–20	Fair	Angels and weepers	Erected by their son, Bishop Blythe of Lichfield, 1503–30; L: long pediment	
		Sawley	P	Prebendary Bothe, d. 1496	Fairly good	—	Quire habit, not mass vestments; L: pediment (long)	128
		Ashover	C, L	Thomas Babyngton, d. 1518	Good, but colour apparently restored	Angels, saints and weepers (the latter in twos and threes hand in hand)	C: ? SS; long gown and scrip	61, 69, 259
		Duffield	K, L	Sir Roger Mynors, d. 1536	Good	Bedesmen	K: SS; L: short pediment and padded sleeves	265
		Fenny Bentley	—	Shrouded effigies of Beresford family	Good	—	—	298
		Scropton	L, K, L	Nicholas Agard, c. 1515	Fairly good; some surface damage	Angels holding shields	L, L: pediment (long); K: chain collar	241
		Bakewell	—	Small tomb without effigy	Fairly good	Seated angels and weepers	—	
		Gt. Cubley	—	No effigy	Poor	Weepers singly and in pairs	By Harper and Moorecock of Burton	8
		Chesterfield	—	No effigy	Fair	Weepers singly and in pairs	By Harper and Moorecock of Burton	
Devon	II	Haccombe	C	Small effigy of young boy, about 2 ft. 2 in. long	Fair	—	Angels and cushions	75
	III	Exeter	Bp	Bishop Stafford, d. 1419	Somewhat worn	—	Canopy over head	197
		Horwood	L	c. 1450	Fair	—	Small figures of her children beside her skirt; horned head-dress	226
	IV	Modbury	K	—	Rather worn	—	Collar of roses only	

County	No.	Place	Figures	Person, date	Condition	Tomb	Remarks	Refs
Dorset	III	Wimborne	K, L	Duke and Duchess of Somerset, d. 1444 (John Beaufort, grandson of John of Gaunt, and grandfather of Henry VII)	Fairly good	—	K: SS; O; angels and cushion / L: SS; small coronet over veil; hands clasped	81
	IV	Marnhull	L, K, L	—	Fair except for a few breakages	—	K: Y / L: butterfly head-dresses with large flap	233
		Puddletown	K	c. 1470	Fairly good	Purbeck tomb with canopy	Y: wearing salet; shield on left side probably modern	97, 214
		Melbury Sampford	K	c. 1470	Very good	Purbeck tomb	Y: wearing salet ornamented with ridges and bosses	231
		Melbury Sampford	K	c. 1470	Very good	Purbeck tomb	Y: almost duplicate of above	227
		Stourton Caundle	L	Widow, c. 1460–70	Fair; broken at feet		Small figures of children in folds of skirt, much broken; barbe and veil	
	v	Puddletown	K, L	c. 1470–80	Poor	Angels holding shields; those of back set in wall over tomb	L: butterfly	
		Netherbury	K	—	Much broken; arms and legs gone	—	SS; long hair	
Durham	II	Durham	Bp	Bishop Hatfield, d. 1381	Much worn	—	Borders of chasuble, etc., were richly ornamented	124
		Durham	K, L	Ralph, Lord Nevill, d. 1367	Mutilated	—	—	
		Durham	K, L	John, Lord Nevill, d. 1388	Mutilated	—	—	
		Dalton-le-Dale	K	Sir William Bowes, c. 1420	Moderate	—	—	
		Staindrop	L, K, L	Ralph Nevill, Earl of Westmorland, d. 1425	Fair; good except for initials	Panels with empty niches	K: SS; O / L, L: hair bunched over ears; coronets. Clerks at desks (headless) at feet	93, 104, 146
	III	Redmarshall	K, L	Thomas de Langton, d. 1440	K: much worn / L: rather better	—	K: SS / L: horned head-dress	
Essex	II	Colne Priory. See Bures (Suffolk) Layer Marney	K	Sir Wm. Marney, d. 1360	Fairly good	Elaborate tomb panels and shields	Arms on jupon	23, 102
	III	Colne Priory. See Bures (Suffolk) Dunmow Priory	K, L	c. 1460–70	Good except feet of K broken	—	K: SS. Good example of very elaborate ridged armour and big elbow and knee cops / L: horned head-dress, approaching butterfly type; collar roses (?)	212
	IV	Dunmow Priory	L	c. 1480	Fair	Panels and shields	Flapped truncated head-dress; necklace with pendants	283
	v	Wethersfield	K, L	c. 1490	Fair	Panels and shields	K: in tabard / L: Y; flapped head-dress	118, 122
Gloucester	i	Gloucester	King	Edward II, d. 1327	Good	Fine stone canopy	Curled hair and crown; cushion and angels; feet on lion	121, 123
		Tewkesbury	K, L	Sir Hugh Despenser, d. 1349	Fair	Fine stone canopy	K: round-topped bascinet; feet on lion / L: framed head-dress; tasselled cushion	113
	II	Berkeley	K, L	Thomas, Lord Berkeley, d. 1364	Fair; hands, noses etc. restored	Shields in quatrefoils	L: framed frilled head-dress	
		Newent	K, L	c. 1370	Worn; arms gone	Shields in quatrefoils	L: framed head-dress	
	IV	Gloucester	P	Abbot Seabroke, d. 1457	Fair	—	Mitre and mass vestments; feet on lion	127

County	Class	Place	Description	Usual attribution (not guaranteed)	State of preservation	Tomb chest	Special features	Illustration
Gloucester	v	Berkeley	K, K	James, Lord Berkeley, d. 1463, and his son; tomb looks c. 1490	Fair; hands, noses etc. patched	Quatrefoils and shields; saints	Y; Y (?)	50
Hampshire	II	Gloucester, St Mary Redcliffe	P	Abbot Parker, d. 1535	Fair	—	Mitre; angels and cushion (broken)	290
		Bristol, St Mary Redcliffe	P	Called William Canynge, d. 1474, c. 1490	Good	—	Looks like a portrait; quire habit; angels at cushion; feet on bearded man	291
		Winchester	Bp	Bp Edington, d. 1366	Fair; hands and feet broken	—	Broken angels at cushion	125
	IV	Winchester	Bp	Bp William of Wykeham, d. 1404	Very good; much colour preserved	Arcaded without figures	Three clerks at feet; angels at cushion	162, 163, 193
		Christchurch	K, L	Sir J. Chideock, d. 1446	K: fair but worn in places; L: poor	—	K: SS	
	v	Godshill (I. of W.)	K, L	Sir John Leigh, d. 1522	Fairly good (possibly repaired in places)	—	L: horned head-dress; L: pedimental (long); K: SS; bedesmen at soles of feet	238
Hereford	II	Hereford	K	Sir Richard Pembridge, d. 1375 (fought at Poitiers)	Fair; right leg renewed	—	Garter below left knee; crest feathers	
		King's Pyon	K	—	Arms and legs broken	—	Placed beside a stone L	
	III	Weobley	K	—	Much worn; arms gone	—	SS; O	
		Weobley	K, L	Sir John Marbury, d. 1437	Much broken but heads good	—	K: SS; O; IHS on bascinet; L: SS; crespine head-dress; SS (?); O	89
		Bredwardine	K	? Sir Roger Vaughan (killed at Agincourt 1415)	Poor	—		
	IV	Hereford	Bp	Bp Stanbery, d. 1474	Fair; a little worn	Angels and weepers	Broken angels at cushion	189
		Burghill	K, L	Sir John Milbourne, c. 1450	Rather worn	Angels and Madonna at end	K: salet; O	
		Kington	K, L	—	Restored (faces, hands, feet, etc. all new)	Angels holding shields	K: Y; L: horned head-dress; L: flapped head-dress	
	v	Stoke Edith	L	c. 1510–20	Bad	—	Butterfly	
		Eye	K		Fairly good (fingers and toe broken)	—	SS	255
	VI	Hereford	P, C, L	Dean John Harvey, d. 1500	Much worn	Angels, saints, weepers, etc.; Annunciation (family kneeling behind angel)	—	297
		Ross		Judge William Rudhall, d. 1529	Fairly good		Judge wears coif; L: pediment head-dress (short)	52, 63, 295
	VI	Eye	K, L	? Sir George Cornwall, d. 1563 (looks rather earlier)	Fairly good	Kneeling weepers; first suggestions of Flemish Renaissance in details	K: SS; tabard; L: Queen of Scots cap; padded sleeves	254
		Hereford	K, L	Sir Alexander Denton, d. 1566	Good	Renaissance panels of Burton type	—	
		Holme Lacy	K, L	John Scudamore, c. 1550	Good; some repairs	Weepers; Renaissance detail	K: chains round neck; L: short pediment; O: angels and cushion (broken)	
Hertford-shire	II	Royston	K		Much worn			
	VI	Wheathampstead	K, L	Sir John Brocket, d. 1543	K: fair; L: poor		K: bearded; chain collar	

County	No.	Place	Figures	Identity / Date	Condition	Notes	Details	Ref.
Kent	I	Canterbury	Abp	Archbishop Stratford, d. 1348	Chipped and worn in places, but good detail	—	Canopy over head; richly embroidered mitre, stole, etc.; double cushion	184
	II	Canterbury	Abp	Archbishop Courtenay, d. 1396	Fair; hands broken	—	Cushion with angels	192
	III	Canterbury	L, King, Queen	Lady Mohun, c. 1390 / Henry IV, d. 1413: Queen Joan, d. 1437	Bad / Good, but K's fingers and Q's arms broken	Inscription / Angels holding shields	— / Q: SS; canopies over hands; richly jewelled crowns	— / 182, 185
		Canterbury	K, L, K	Earl of Somerset, d. 1410; Margaret Holland, d. 1437; Duke of Clarence, d. 1421 (son of Henry IV)	Good but discoloured	—	K: bearded; looks like a portrait. KK: SS; tabards. All these wear coronets, and have angels by cushions; L and one K have dogs at feet and other K has eagle	190
	IV	Ash	K, L	—	Fairly good	—	K: SS; bald forehead, tabard; angel supports helm. L: widow's barbe	216
		Minster-in-Sheppey	K	c. 1475	Rather worn; arms gone	Now on Purbeck tomb	Y	
	V	Little Chart	K	Sir John Darell, d. 1509	Good	—	SS; directions as to burial here in will	203
	VI	Minster-in-Sheppey	K	Sir Thomas Cheyne, d. 1558	Much worn	Purbeck; Renaissance detail	KG: Garter robes; small ruff	
Lancashire	II	Huyton	P	John de Winwick, d. 1360 (?)	Much worn; very poor	—	Quire habit	
	IV	Halsall	P	c. 1470	Somewhat worn	Crucifixion, angels, saints under pared down canopies. Possibly a collection put together here when church was rebuilt	Amice with pendants	296
		Warrington	K, L	Sir John Butler (or Boteler)	Fairly good		K: plain collar; hands clasped. L: cauls and veil	7
		Ormskirk (said to have come from Burscough Priory)	K, L	a Stanley, c. 1490	Rather poor; legs gone	—	K: chain collar and tabard, on which arms, including Swastika of Man, are carved; long hair. L: coronet over veil	
	V	Halsall	K, L	a Stanley, c. 1490	Poor; legs gone	—	L: coronet over veil / L: tabard ⎫ almost duplicates of foregoing / L: coronet ⎬ / K: tabard	
		Halsall	K, L	c. 1490–1500	K: fair / L: poor and headless	—	K: tabard	
Leicester	II	Leicester, Trinity Hospital	L	? Mary de Bohun (d. 1394) (first wife of Henry IV)	Rather worn	—	Veil	248
		Whitwick	K	Called Sir John Talbot	Surface entirely perished	—	—	
		Kirby Bellars	K	c. 1360–70	Rather worn; arms broken	—	—	
		Kirby Bellars	L	c. 1360–70	Fair; hands broken	—	Widow's veil and barbe	
		Appleby Magna	K, L		Fair; heads worn	—	Rather flat; second-rate work. L: framed	
		Bottesford	K	William, Lord Rous, d. 1414	Good	Angels holding shields	SS; O; Garter; peacock helm under head; fine detail; breastplate indicated under jupon	20, 204

County	Class	Place	Description	Usual attribution (not guaranteed)	State of preservation	Tomb chest	Special features	Illustration
Leicester	III	Bottesford	K	John, Lord Rous, d. 1421	Good	Angels holding shields	SS; O; fine detail	175
		Melton Mowbray	L	—	All interest destroyed by restoration	—	—	
	IV	Lutterworth	C, L	—	Fair, but noses, hands and face of L appear to be restored	Angels holding shields	C: wears long robe over armour / L: veil	
	V	Ashby-de-la-Zouch	C	Pilgrim	Much worn	—	SS; holding staff, with pilgrim's hat ornamented with shell under head; long hair	210
		Leicester, St Mary	Bp	Bp Penny of Carlisle (former Abbot of Leicester), d. 1520	Suspiciously good nose certainly new, smothered in paint	—	—	289
		Thurlaston	K, L	John Turville, c. 1509	Very fair	Angels holding shields	K: SS / L: SS; O over long hair	260
		Lockington	L	Lady Elizabeth Ferrers, c. 1500	Very fair	Bedesmen; angels at ends	Coronet worn over long loose hair	268
		Prestwold / Prestwold	L, L	c. 1520 Incised slab on top	Fair / Fair	Seated bedesmen / Angels and bedesmen	Pediment head-dresses (long)	263
		Castle Donington	K, L	Robert Hazelrig, d. 1529; ? 1536	Very fair	Angels and bedesmen	K: SS; big neck-guards / L: short pediment head-dress and puffed sleeves	262
	VI	Bottesford	K, L	Thomas, 1st Earl of Rutland, d. 1543	Good	Weepers; Renaissance detail	By Richard Parker of Burton; bearded; Garter robes	
		Ashby-de-la-Zouch	K, L	Earl of Huntingdon, d. 1561	Good	Weepers and shields	Bearded; coronets and Garter robes	
		Swepstone	K	—	Fair	—	L: widow	
		Fenny Drayton	—	No effigy; Nicholas Purefoy, d. 1543	Good	Weepers and angels; Burton vase panels	Bearded	
Lincoln	II	Spilsby	K, L	Robert, Lord Willoughby d'Eresby	Much restored; noses, hands, and other projections new and whole scraped	—	K: O / L: three little dogs at feet	302
		Spilsby	K	William, Lord Willoughby d'Eresby ?, c. 1420	Spoilt by restoration; patched and scraped	Tomb chest appears to be entirely new	Band with rosettes round bascinet (if correctly restored). Little figures in niches on each side of slabs; their heads at least are new, but there must have been some grounds for their restoration	
		North Cockerington	K	c. 1370	Bad; a mere torso without head, arms or legs; part of lion at feet remains	—	—	
		Broughton	K, L	Sir H. Redford, d. 1404	Rather worn	—	K: SS; O	
		Stamford, St Mary	K	—	Very worn and broken	—	L: almost crespine	

	III	Wellingore	K, L	—	Rather worn	Panels and shields	K: SS; O L: widow's barbe and veil spread over cauls	
		Harlaxton	C, L	Called Judge Rickhill, *c.* 1410	Fair, but broken and chipped in places	—	C in curious kind of turban or chaperon; houppelande L: crespine head-dress	
	IV	Boston	K	—	Restored, probably incorrectly	Angels holding shields	Restoration has made it difficult to see what this has been	
		Boston	L	—	Restored	—	—	
	V	Leake	K	—	Rather worn	—	—	
Middlesex (including London)	I	Westminster	K	Prince John of Eltham, d. 1337	Fairly good	Weepers cut out and set against black composition background	Coronet and shield; cross-legged; wears short fronted surcoat; cushion and angels	11, 12, 13, 31, 119
	II	Westminster	C, L	Prince William of Windsor and Princess Blanche of the Tower (infant children of Edward III), d. 1340	Much worn; feet of prince cut away	—	Contracted for by John Orchard 1376; cushions; no angels; small effigies only about 1 ft. 6 in. long	74
		Westminster	Abp	Archbishop Simon Langham, Cardinal, d. 1376	Good but angels broken	—	Angels at head; dogs at feet	100, 161
		London, Gt St Helen's	C, L	John Oteswich, *c.* 1400	Good	—	C: bearded; long gown (houppelande) with scrip and short sword at side L: veil; buttons in front	131
	III	St Katharine's Chapel	C, L, L	John Holland, Duke of Exeter, d. 1447	Fairly good, but one wife has new face and a few other patches	Fine stone canopy over	All these wear coronets	171
	IV	London, Gt St Helen's	K, L	Sir John Crosby, d. 1474	Good	—	K: Y L: butterfly with large flaps; elaborate collar	242
	V	Westminster	K, L	Sir Giles Daubeny, K.G., d. 1506	Good	Modern tomb	K: Garter robes; bedesmen at feet L: a kind of O over loose hair	280
Monmouth	III	Abergavenny	K, L	Sir William-ap-Thomas, *c.* 1450	Fair; cracked in places	Made up of fragments collected from tombs or possibly retables; Annunciation; angels; apostles; gablettes	K: SS; O L: horned head-dress	48, 80
	V	Abergavenny	K, L	Sir Richard Herbert, *c.* 1470	Fair	Saints and angels made up with alien fragments; gablettes	K: Y L: O over loose hair	51
		Abergavenny	K	Sir Richard Herbert, d. 1510	Fair	Seated angels and bedesmen; assumption and kneeling weepers set in niche over tomb	SS; mutilated inscription	9
		Newport	K	—	Bad	—	—	
Norfolk	II	East Harling	K, L	*c.* 1370	K: good but hands broken L: fair	Placed on later tomb	L: framed head-dress K: unicorn on jupon	133, 134
	III	Ashwellthorpe	K, L	Sir Edmund de Thorpe, d. 1417	Good	Angels holding shields	K: SS; O L: SS; crespine head-dress; dogs at feet	84, 85
	V	Norwich	Bp	Bp Goldwell, d. 1499	Much worn	—	Feet on lion	
	?	Castle Acre	—	—	Fragment	—	—	
North-ampton	I	Ashton	K	Johan de Herteshull, d. 1365	Much broken	—	Inscription	130
	II	Orlingbury	K	*c.* 1370	Fair	—	—	
		Spratton	K	Sir John Swinford, d. 1371	Good	—	SS; (the earliest SS collar); jupon laced at side	143

County	Class	Place	Description	Usual attribution (not guaranteed)	State of preservation	Tomb chest	Special features	Illustration
North-ampton	III	Lowick	K, L	Ralph Greene, d. 1419	Good	Angels holding shields	K: O; stag crest; fauld looks like square plates covered with leather; L: crespine head-dress; hands clasped; canopy over heads; contract preserved	5, 19, 180
	IV	Yelvertoft	P	—	Rather worn	—	Mass vestments	288
		Dodford	K	Sir John Cressy, d. 1444	Good	Angels holding shields; fine shield of arms at end	SS. Inscription	27, 73, 215
	V	Greene's Norton	K, L	Sir Thomas Greene, d. 1457	Fair, but K's legs gone	—	K: SS; L: SS; horned head-dress	—
		Irthlingborough	C, L	c. 1490	Bad	—	Long pediment	105, 209
		Irthlingborough	L	c. 1490	Very poor	—	—	
		Gt Addington	K	c. 1490	Fair		SS	
		Lowick	K	Earl of Wiltshire, d. 1498	Good	Shields in panels	SS; tabard; long hair; bedesmen against soles of feet. Inscription	
		Fawsley	K, L	Sir Richard Knightley, d. 1534	Perfect	Weepers set against black background	K: SS; fine tabard L: pediment head-dress (short); much colour preserved	58, 60, 274
		Deene	L, C, L	Sir Robert Brudenell, d. 1531 (Chief Justice of Common Pleas)	Good	Renaissance detail and shields in panels	L: pediment head-dress (short) C: Judge's coif; much colour preserved; Judge's robe red	301
		Upton	K, L	Sir Richard Knightley, d. 1537 (probably made in his lifetime)	Rather worn	—	L: widow's veil and barbe K: SS; tabard	293
		Apethorpe	K	Sir Richard Dalton, d. 1442 (?) (looks c. 1500)	—	—	L: loose hair under round cap with wreath Small effigy 3 ft. 9½ in. long; tabard; slab 5 ft. 9½ in.; Coronation of Virgin placed over his head	79
	VI	Stanford-on-Avon	K, L	Sir Thomas Cave, d. 1558	Good	Kneeling family; Renaissance detail	K: chain collar L: Queen of Scots cap; puffed sleeves and shoulders	304, 305
North-umberland	IV	Chillingham	K, L	Sir Ralph Grey, d. 1443	Good, but faces, etc. have been touched up	Elaborate stone tomb with figures of saints	K: tabard; ladder and cloak badges all round slab	
	V	Bothal	K, L	Ralph, Lord Ogle, d. 1513	Much worn	Weepers	L: horned head-dress	
Nottingham	II	Willoughby-in-the-Wolds	C	Sir Richard Willoughby, d. 1362 (but looks rather later), Chief Justice	Fairly good; top of head mended	—	K: tabard and chain collar	166
		Willoughby-in-the-Wolds	K	Sir Richard Willoughby	Fair (face may be touched up)		L: flapped truncated head-dress Houppelande with high collar	
		Strelley	K, L	Sir Sampson Strelley, d. 1391 (looks a little later)	Good (but possibly touched up in places)	Angels holding shields	—	150
		Hoveringham	K, L	Sir J. Goushill, d. 1403 and Dowager Duchess of Norfolk (killed at Battle of Shrewsbury)	Rather worn	—	K: mail and collar not worked; holds horn; Saracen's head crest L: coronet and cauls; early form of crespine; hands clasped K: SS; O; swelling breastplate under jupon; hands clasped	

Co.	Pl.	Place	Fig.	Name / Date	Condition	Accessories	Description	Pages
		Whatton	K	Sir Adam de Newmarch, c. 1380	Worn; leg broken	—	O; plate armour seems indicated under jupon	142
		Nuttall	K	Sir Robert Cokefield	Good	—	Jupon laced at side	140
		Fledborough	K	Sir Gervase Clifton (?)	Bad; legs gone	—	Feet on lion	141, 236
		Clifton	L	Dame Alice Clifton (Nevill), wife of above	Fairly good	—	Net and veil	
	III	Holme Pierrepont, St Mary's, Nottingham	K		Good	—	—	
		Nottingham, St Mary's	C	John Salmon (Mayor 1383, d. 1416)	A mere fragment Mutilated fragment	Trinity, Madonna; angels holding shields	Curious high hat	195
		Willoughby-in-the-Wolds	K, L	Sir Hugh Willoughby, d. 1448	Much worn	—	K: O; wears early form of salet; L: horned head-dress; feet on dogs	16, 88, 158
		Worksop	L	—	K: good; L: fairly good	—	Cauls	
		Southwell	Bp	c. 1450	Very poor	—	—	
	IV	Sutton Bonington	K	c. 1470	Bad	—	Y	
		Strelley	K, L	John Strelley, d. 1501	Fair, but worn in parts	Panels and stone canopy over. Inscription	K: chain collar; L: flapped truncated head-dress	270
	VI	Holme Pierrepont	K	Sir Henry Pierrepont, d. 1499	Good	Panels	Y; will directed 'a tomb of alabaster to be set upon his sepulchre and graven by the discretion of his executors'	87, 246, 257
		Ratcliffe-on-Soar	K, L	Ralph Sacheverell, d. 1539	Very good	Panels. Inscription	K: SS; L: pediment head-dress (short)	77, 110, 247
		Ratcliffe-on-Soar	K, L		Good, but L's hands broken	Weepers holding shields. Inscription	—	
Oxford	II	Dorchester	K	c. 1390	Fair	—	Band round bascinet	1, 153
		Northleigh	K, L	Sir William Wilcote, d. 1411	Good	—	K: SS; O; L: SS; high collar and crespine head-dress; houppelande	
	III	Broughton	L / K	Called Lady Wykeham, but looks earlier than K; Sir Thomas Wykeham	Restored in 1846; Restored; hand, legs, etc. new	—	SS; crespine head-dress; Y. It seems doubtful whether this Yorkist K and Lancastrian L have been rightly put together	177
	IV	Stanton Harcourt	K, L	Sir Robert Harcourt, K.G., d. 1471	Good, but colour badly renewed; hands new	Panels and shields	K: Y; Garter robes; L: widow's veil and barbe; Garter on left arm	49, 219
	V	Minster Lovell	K	Lord Lovell	Fair	Weepers and saints	Veil and barbe; coronet; Garter on left wrist	28, 82, 183
		Ewelme	L	Alice, Duchess of Suffolk, d. 1477	Good	Angels (cadaver under)	—	
		North Aston	K, L	c. 1490	Good	Angels and bedesmen	K: SS; L: flapped truncated head-dress	34, 240
		Chipping Norton	K, L	Richard Croft, d. 1502	Fairly good	—	K: chain collar; L: pedimental head-dress with long flaps at side	253
		Oxford, St Aldate's	P	John Noble, d. 1522 (Principal of Broadgates Hall, afterwards Pembroke College)	Fair	Angels	University hood over shoulder	294
		Stanton Harcourt	K	c. 1490	Fairly good; new nose and hands disfigured by repainting	(? alabaster)	SS	

County	Class	Place	Description	Usual attribution (not guaranteed)	State of preservation	Tomb chest	Special features	Illustration
Rutland	III	Burley	K, L	—	Mutilated; K's legs gone	—	K: SS; O	
	v	Exton	K, L	Sir John Harrington, d. 1524	Good	—	L: horned; collar ? SS very worn. Inscription. K: collar with motto	225
		Ashwell	P	—	Fair (hands, toes, and angels broken)	—	L: pediment head-dress with long flaps. Eucharistic vestments	
Shropshire	II	Tong	K, L	Sir Fulke Pembrugge, d. 1409	Fair	—	K: O	
		Kinlet	L	c. 1410	Fairly good	—	L: veil and barbe. Baby beside her in swaddling clothes; crespine head-dress with plain band across forehead	
	III	Burford	L	?Princess Elizabeth (daughter of John of Gaunt), d. 1426	Fairly good; nose new	Saints and angels	Coronet over flowing hair	249
		Tong	K, L	Sir Richard Vernon, d. 1451	Very good	Weepers and Annunciation	K: SS; O; horse-head crest	70, 181
	v	Kinlet	K, L	Sir Humphrey Blount, d. 1478	Fairly good		L: horned head-dress; fine detail. K: Y	
		Tong	K, L	Richard Vernon, d. 1517	Fair	Weepers and bedesmen in elaborate niches. Inscription	L: butterfly with large flap. K: SS	42, 252
		Shrewsbury Abbey	K, L	William Charlton, d. 1529	Fair, but covered with dark paint; K's head looks new	Angels and bedesmen	L: pediment (long type). Inscription	25, 36
		Newport	C, L	c. 1530–40	Fairly good	Angels, weepers and bedesmen; twisted shafts at corners	L: pediment (long type)	300
	vi	Kinlet	K, L	Sir John Blount, d. 1531	Good	Weepers in groups; Renaissance detail; inscription	L: pediment (short)	
		Wroxeter	C, L	Lord Chief Justice Bromley, d. 1555	Good	Weepers; Renaissance detail; child holding flower	K: SS. L: pediment (short)	62
Somerset	II	Wells	Bp	Bp Ralph, d. 1363	Fair; a little worn and scratched	—	C in Judge's coif. L: pediment (short); pheasant beside cushion	303
	III	Wells	Bp	Bp Harewell, d. 1386	Fair		Rich detail	191
		Wells	P	c. 1440	Fair, but broken in places		Hares at feet. Broken angels at cushion	103, 126
		Porlock	K, L	Sir Hugh Luttrell, d. 1428	Very fair	Annunciation and priests alternating with shields	K: SS; O; angels supports helm	32, 47, 160
		Dunster	K, L	c. 1440	Poor; K's legs gone	Lofty stone canopy	L: horned	172
	IV	Glastonbury	C	A lay bursar of the Abbey, c. 1470	Very fair	Stone tomb with angels and heraldry in panels	K: SS; O	211
		Yatton	C, L	Sir Richard Newton, d. 1449 and second wife, d. 1475	Very fair	Angels	C: Judge's coif; robe and pouch. L: butterfly with flap. Date apparently that of death of wife	292

County	No.	Place		Person	Condition	Stone cadaver under	Description	Pages
Stafford	I	Wells	Bp	Bp Beckyngton, d. 1465	Rather worn	—	Tomb erected 1451. Collar of roses alone; butterfly	194
		Ilton	L	c. 1470	Fair	—	The first alabaster knight; mail and surcoat; shield; legs crossed; drawing sword; head on cushion with angels	229
		Hanbury	K	Sir John de Hanbury, c. 1300	Fairly good	—	K: SS; O; angels at helm as well as cushion of L	117
	II	Elford	K, L	Sir John Arderne (?), d. 1408	Good, but restored by Richardson, c. 1852	Angels and weepers	L: early type of crespine	38, 149
		Elford	K	—	Much restored by Richardson	—	Inscription as restored gives name of Sir Thomas Stanley and date 1470 which is impossible (? 1370)	—
	V	Audley	K	—	Rather poor	—	Cross-legged (unique at this date); seems to have held a shield	26, 179, 256
		Burton-on-Trent (Museum)	K	—	A mutilated fragment	—		
		Elford	L, K, L	Sir William Smythe, d. 1525 and wives (Isabella Nevill, niece of the King-maker and Anne Staunton)	Good, but cleverly restored	Bedesmen in elaborate niches. Inscription	K: SS / L: coronet over flowing hair / L: pediment (long	
		Tamworth	K, L	Sir John Ferrers, d. 1512	Fair, but hands and faces damaged	Weepers mostly headless	K: SS / L: pediment (long)	
	VI	Leigh	K, L	c. 1523	Fair, but worn in places	Weepers in pairs and angels much broken. Inscription	K: collar of roses only / L: short pediment	68
		Clifton Campville	C, L	Sir John Vernon, d. 1545	Good	Weepers and seated bedesmen, etc.; twisted shafts; inscription; frieze of animals and birds on base	K: flat cap and chain collar / L: short pediment and rosary at side	
Suffolk	II	Bures, St Edmund's Chapel (from Colne Priory)	K	a De Vere, Earl of Oxford, c. 1370	Goo[d]	Weepers in pairs (one angel from later tomb incorporated in restored monument)	Star of de Veres carved on jupon	30, 139
	III	Bures, St Edmund's Chapel (from Colne Priory)	K, L	a De Vere, Earl of Oxford, c. 1420	Fairly good	Angels holding shields	K: SS; O / L: ? SS; horned head-dress. These two tombs were recently in a private house at Earls Colne, but on its sale have been re-erected in the little chapel at Bures	164
		Dennington	K, L	Lord Bardolf, K.G., d. 1441	Good	Empty niches	K: SS; O; Garter; feet on hawk; feather crest / K: SS; horned; feet on wyvern	112, 176, 178
	V	Wingfield	K, L	John de la Pole, Duke of Suffolk d. 1491 and Elizabeth Plantagenet (sister of Edward IV)	Duke good. Duchess fair	—	Duke: coronet; Garter and Garter robes; fine Saracen's head crest on helm / Duchess: coronet and veil	108, 275
		Chilton	K, L	Robert Crane, d. 1500	Fairly good; L's arms broken	—	K: tabard; unicorn at feet / L: SS; flapped head-dress	282
		Chilton	C	George Crane, d. 1491	Fairly good	—	Long robe and scrip; flat hat and liripipe over shoulders	269
Surrey	IV	Lingfield	K, L	Reginald, Lord Cobham, d. 1446 (fought at Agincourt) and Anne (Bardolf), 2nd wife, d. 1453	Good	—	Saracen's head crest on helm / L: veil and widow's barbe. Will preserved directing body to be placed here before high altar	111, 116, 205

County	Class	Place	Descrip-tion	Usual attribution (not guaranteed)	State of preservation	Tomb chest	Special features	Illustration
Sussex	III	Arundel	C, L	Thomas, Earl of Arundel, d. 1416 and wife Beatrix (daughter of John I of Portugal)	Good	Monks or canons; original metal hearse	Gablets and canopies over heads; C: SS; coronet and long robe; L: coronet over very elaborate crespine head-dress; dogs at feet	6, 101, 138, 188
	v	Arundel	K	John FitzAlan, Earl of Arundel, d. 1435	Fair	Stone cadaver under	SS; tabard; close fitting bascinet with holes for fixing vizor; angels and cushions	271
		Chichester	Bp	Bp Storey, d. 1503	Much worn			
		Chichester	Bp	Bp Shirburne, d. 1536	Good (? somewhat restored)	Panels; angels supporting shield in niche above tomb	Angels at head and lion at feet	198
Warwick	I	Easebourne	K	Sir David Owen, d. 1542	Fairly good	—	Collar SS and roses; tabard. Tomb ordered 40 years before death as explained in will	272
		Kingsbury	K	c. 1360	Bad; little more than a lump of alabaster	—	Seems to have been lying on side and to have had a shield, but details almost obliterated	
	II	Warwick	K, L	Thomas Beauchamp, Earl of Warwick, d. 1371 (one of leaders at Crécy and Poitiers)	Fairly good; new noses	Weepers	Breastplate indicated under jupon; hands clasped; both heads on cushions with angels; K: feet on bear; L: framed head-dress	29, 33, 37, 148
		Aston	K	c. 1370	Fairly good	—	Ornamented band on front of bascinet; now placed on tomb beside a stone L of c. 1490	
		Birmingham	K	Sir John de Birmingham	Fairly good (rather blackened)	Arcade; no figures	Band round bascinet	
	III	Meriden	K	Sir John Wyard, d. 1404	Good	—	Richly decorated sword; arms on jupon; angels by cushions; hip-belt with rosettes	157, 232
		Merevale	K, L	? Edmund, Lord Ferrers of Chartley, c. 1440	Fairly good	Angels	K: O; an early form of salet; feather crest; L: horned; dogs at feet	21, 99, 170
		Wootton Wawen	K	John Harewell, c. 1428	Fairly good	—	Band round bascinet; chain collar; feet on dog	168
	IV	Polesworth	L	Isabel Cockayne, d. 1447	Fair	Shields	Crespine	155
		Aston	K, L	Sir Thomas Erdington, d. 1433 and wife, d. 1460	Fairly good	Angels	K: ? SS (apparently obliterated); L: ? SS; butterfly; Y	
		Astley	K	a Harcourt, c. 1462	Good	—	SS	
	v	Grendon		Sir E. Gray, Lord Ferrers of Groby, d. 1457	Fairly good	—	Butterfly	
		Birmingham	P	c. 1460	Restored	—	Quire habit	
		Astley	L	c. 1500	Very fair	—	collar roses only	
		Astley	L	Elizabeth, Lady L'Isle, d. 1483	Very fair	—	Loose hair and circlet } Now on same tomb as Lord Ferrers	251
		Astley	L	Marchioness of Dorset (?), d. 1530	Rather broken	—	Long pediment }	
		Coleshill	K, L	Sir Simon Digby, d. 1519	Good	Panels and shields	K: SS; L: pediment (long). Inscription	285
		Compton Winyates	L	Sir William Compton, 1528	Bad; lower portion only	—		
		Compton Winyates	K		Poor; legs gone	—	SS; tabard	

County		Place		Person & date	Condition	Renaissance type	Description	Page
	VI	Monks' Kirby	K, L	Sir William Fielding, d. 1547 and wife Elizabeth, d. 1539	Fairly good; nose and toes new	—	Inscription. Slightly bald / L: short pedimental and ruff / It is possible that the K is an older effigy modified and recut to adapt it	286
		Coventry, St Michael	K, L, C	Thomas Essex, Elizabeth Swillington, d. 1546; Ralph Swillington, d. 1525 (Attorney General, 1524)	Fairly good	Renaissance type. Inscription	K: bearded; chain collar / L: short pediment / C: long gown and chain collar	
	II	Coleshill	K, L	John Digby (d. 1558)	Fairly good	Inscription	—	
	IV	Alcester	Bp	Fulke Greville (d. 1559)	Good	Inscription	—	
Wiltshire	V	Salisbury	K	Bishop Mitford, d. 1407	Fair; foot broken	Empty niches	(? might be marble)	220, 239
		Salisbury	K	Lord John Hungerford, d. 1459	Fairly good	—	SS; angels and cushion	266
		Salisbury	K	Sir John Cheyney, d. 1509 (Henry VII's standard-bearer at Battle of Bosworth)		—	SS; Garter robes; long hair; angels and cushions	
	III	Bromham	K	Richard Beauchamp, Lord St Amand, d. 1508	Fair, except for initials	Purbeck	SS; beavor and cap; huge neck-guard	284
Worcester		Bromsgrove	K, L	Sir N. Stafford, c. 1450	Fairly good	—	K: SS; O; boar's head crest / L: horned	91
		Bromsgrove	L	—	Fair	—	Long loose hair and circlet	250
	IV	Kidderminster	K, L	Sir Hugh Cokesay, c. 1445	Rather worn	Angels holding shields and tracery panels	K: SS; tabard and ridged salet with raised vizor / L: horned	230
		Martley	K, L	Sir Hugh Mortimer, c. 1459	Rather worn	—	Y	
	V	Stanford-on-Teme	K, L	Sir Humphrey Selway, d. 1493	Fair; L's head not guaranteed	Kneeling weepers, 3 grouped at end	K: SS / L: truncated. Inscription	65
	VI	Bromsgrove	L, K, L	Sir John Talbot, d. 1501 (looks more like 1550), probably erected on death of 2nd wife	Fair	Panels and shields. Inscription	K: short pediment / K: SS / L: Queen of Scots cap	
Yorkshire	I	York	C	Prince William of Hatfield, d. 1346	Worn on top	—	Short embroidered jupon and long cloak with dagged edges; cushion and angels; about 4 ft. 6 in. long; feet on lion	120
	II	West Tanfield	K, L	Sir John Marmion, d. 1386	Fairly good except hands	Iron hearse	K: SS; jewelled band; feather crest; arms on jupon	154
		Hornby	K, L	Sir John Conyers, d. 1422	Fair; K's legs broken	—	L: close fitting cap; feet on long-tailed ape(?)	165
		Swine	K, L	Sir Robert Hilton, d. 1372	Good except broken arms	Broken weeper and shields	L: veil / K: chaplets of Lascelles on jupon; feather crest on helm	96, 144
		Swine	K, L	? Sir Robert Hilton, c. 1410	Good	—	L: veil and wimple / K: SS; O / L: veil over cauls	14, 109, 159
		Swine	K, L	a Hilton, c. 1410	Fairly good	Angels in pairs holding shields	K: chaplets of Lascelles on jupon; good example of arm and leg armour / O: chaplets on jupon; very like those above	
		Pickering	K, L	Sir David Roucliffe, d. 1407	Much worn and broken	Angels in pairs holding shields	K: SS; O / L: SS	145
		Pickering	K	c. 1380	A mere fragment; almost destroyed	—	—	

County	Class	Place	Description	Usual attribution (not guaranteed)	State of preservation	Tomb chest	Special features	Illustration
Yorkshire		Selby	K	John, Lord Darcy, d. 1411	A worn fragment; a mere torso	Angels holding shields	SS	132
	III	Hull	C, L	Sir William de la Pole, d. 1366 / 1410	Fair	—	C: bearded; long cloak / L: veil	
		Darfield	K, L	c. 1410	Moderate	—	K: SS	
		Harewood	K, L	Sir Richard Redman, d. 1426. These were buried elsewhere but the church was rebuilt c. 1430 and it is suggested that this and the following tomb were then erected in memory of ancestors	Fairly good	Seated angels holding shields	L: net over hair; angels by cushion / K: SS; O; horse-head crest; eagle buckle on hip-belt / L: crespine; feet on dogs	17, 92, 147
		Harewood	K, L	Sir William Ryther, d. 1425	K: fair / L: Poor	Angels holding shields	K: SS; O } similar to above / L: crespine }	15, 167
		Harewood	C, L	Sir William Gascoigne (Judge), d. 1419	Good		Judge: close fitting coif and long robe / L: crespine	
		Methley	K, L	Sir Robert Waterton, d. 1424	Good	Trinity; seated angels and shields	K: SS; bearded with very large O, looking like a turban	18, 90, 186
		Wadworth	K, L	Sir Edmund FitzWilliam, d. 1430	Moderate	Angels holding shields (mostly headless)	L: SS; crespine (elaborate jewelling) / K: SS; O	
		Barmston	K	c. 1420	Fairly good	Angels holding shields and tracery panels	L: veil over cauls / O; sacred name on bascinet	
	IV	Wentworth	K, L	a Gascoigne, c. 1460	K: poor / L: very bad	Weepers (separate now)	K: SS; tabard	24
		Harewood	K, L	a Gascoigne, c. 1470	Good	Weepers	K: Y / L: veil and widow's barbe	94, 207
		Harewood	K, L	Sir John Nevill of Womersley, d. 1482	Good, except K's face rather worn	Angels and weepers	K: collar looks like SOSOS (?); tabard; bull's head crest / L: veil and widow's barbe	114, 222
		Burton Agnes	K, L	Sir Walter Griffith, d. 1481	Very fair	Saints and angels	K: SS; feet on griffin / L: SS; veil over loose hair; small figures of son and daughter on either side	55, 221
		Eastrington	C, L	Sir John Portington, d. 1462	C: poor / L: bad	—	Judge's coif and robes worn over armour	
		Methley	K, L	Lord Welles, K.G., d. 1461 (killed at battle of Towton)	Fairly good	Angels	K: chain collar, tabard and garter / L: chain collar; horned head-dress with wide forehead band	223
		Ryther	K	Sir William Ryther, d. 1475	Fairly good	Weepers	Y; elaborate standard of mail	56, 196, 235
		Thornhill	K, L	Sir John Savill, d. 1481	Fairly good	Weepers	K: Y / L: circlet over loose hair	67, 234
		Halsham	K	—	Fairly good	Angels	SS; rolled hair	208

	Place	C	Subject	Condition	Trinity, angels, etc.	Details	
v	Sheriff Hutton	C	Edward, Prince of Wales (?), d. 1484	Poor	Trinity, angels, etc.	Crown; looks earlier than date assigned, but difficult to judge owing to poor condition	267
	South Cowton	K	Sir Richard Conyers, d. 1493	Fairly good	—	SS and roses; band over hair	224
	South Cowton	L	—	Fairly good	—	Flapped truncated head-dress	115
	South Cowton	L	—	Fairly good	—	O over loose hair	
	Harewood	K, L	Sir Richard Redman, d. 1476 (?) (but looks about 20 years later)	Very good	Saints and angels	K: SS and roses; L: widow's veil and barbe; bedesman on lion at feet of K	53, 54, 95, 107, 243
	Batley	K, L	Sir William Mirfield, d. 1496	Fair	Stone weepers	L: O over loose hair	261
	Allerton Mauleverer	K, L	Sir John Mauleverer, d. 1458 (?)	Very poor	—	K: beavor	
VI	Whitkirk	K, L	Sir Robert Scargill, d. 1531 (looks a little later) (fought at Flodden)	Fairly good	Weepers; semi-classical details. Inscription	Inscription; L: Queen of Scots cap and frills at wrists; Seems to have been erected under provisions of will of his wife, c. 1546-7	
Wales							
II	Montgomery	K	—	Bad; restored in stone and painted over	—	Chain round bascinet	
	Penmynydd (Anglesey)	K, L	c. 1410	Fair	Empty niches and shields	K: fluted bascinet; angels by cushions; small shield on camail over chin; breastplate indicated under jupon	135
IV	Beaumaris (near Llandegai Bangor)	K, L	—	Fair	Saints	L: crespine; large string of buttons	136
	Slebech (new church)	K, L	William Griffith of Penrhyn, d. 1480	Rather worn	Angels holding shields	K: Y; L: butterfly with flap	
	Ruabon	K, L	Sir Henry Wogan	Worn; L's face looks new		K: Y; L: O over loose hair	
v		K, L	John ap Elis Eyton, d. 1526 (joined Henry VII before Bosworth)	Fair; weepers and faces worn	Angels and saints	K: SS; L: short pediment; Inscription	
	Llandaff	K	Sir David Mathew (standard-bearer of Edward IV at Towton) (looks c. 1490-1500)	Fair; face rather damaged	—	—	
	Llandaff	L	Sir Christopher Mathew (d. 1500) and wife (1526)	Rather worn	Two angels out of place	Widow's veil and barbe	299
	Llandaff	K, L		Fairly good	Weepers (rather mutilated)	K: SS; L: short pediment; Inscription	
	Llandaff	K, L	Sir William Mathew (d. 1528) and wife (1530)	Fairly good	Angels and bedesmen	K: SS; L: short pediment; Inscription	
	Montgomery	K	Stone effigy now on it of Thomas Whyte, d. 1482	Restored in stone and painted over	—	—	
	Tenby	—		—	Saints with family in adoration	—	

2. Tutbury Doorway (Staffs). First use of alabaster
3. Bakewell (Derby). Sir Godfrey Foljambe, d. 1376
4. Youlgreave (Derby). Robert Gylbert, d. 1492

5. Lowick (Northants). Tomb of Ralph Greene, d. 1419

6. Arundel (Sussex). Tomb of Thomas, Earl of Arundel, d. 1416

7. Warrington (Lancs). Tomb of Sir John Butler
8. Great Cubley (Derby). Weepers

9. Abergavenny (Mon). Tomb of Sir Richard Herbert, d. 1510
10. Norbury (Derby). Tomb of Ralph Fitzherbert, d. 1483

11. Westminster. Head of Prince John of Eltham, d. 1337
12.   „   } Weepers of Prince John of Eltham
13.   „

14. Swine (Yorks). Knight of Hilton family. Weepers
15. Harewood (Yorks). Tomb of Sir Wm Gascoigne

16. Willoughby-in-the-Wolds (Notts). Weepers
17. Harewood (Yorks). Angel
18. Methley (Yorks). Side of tomb chest

19. Lowick (Northants)   20. Bottesford (Leics)
21. Merevale (Warw)   22. Ashbourne (Derby)

ANGEL-WEEPERS

23. Layer Marney (Essex). Tomb of Sir Wm Marney, d. 1360
24. Barmston (Yorks). Tomb c. 1420

25. Tong (Salop). Tomb of Richard Vernon, d. 1517
26. Elford (Staffs). Tomb of Sir Wm Smythe, d. 1524

27. Dodford (Northants). Angels from tomb of Sir John Cressy
28. Ewelme (Oxon). Angels from tomb of Duchess of Suffolk

29. Warwick. Weepers from tomb of Thomas Beauchamp,
Earl of Warwick, d. 1371
30. Bures (Suff), from Colne Priory. Weepers from tomb of
Earl of Oxford

31. Westminster   32. Wells (Som)   33. Warwick
34. North Aston (Oxon)   35. Norbury (Derby)   36. Tong (Salop)

WEEPERS (MALE)

37. Warwick   38. Elford (Staffs)   39. Norbury (Derby)
40. Windsor (Berks)   41. Aldermaston (Berks)   42. Kinlet (Salop)

WEEPERS (FEMALE)

43. Weepers. Haversham (Bucks)
44.   „   Norbury (Derby)

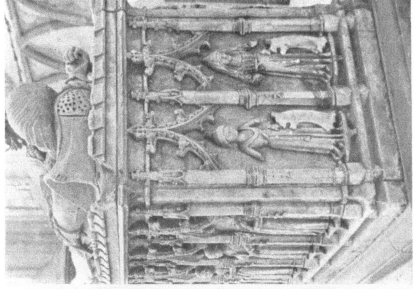

46. Weepers. Norbury (Derby)

45. Weepers. Ashbourne (Derby)

47. Wells (Som) 48. Abergavenny (Mon) 49. Minster Lovell (Oxon)

50. Berkeley (Glouc) 51. Abergavenny (Mon) 52. Ross (Heref)

WEEPERS (SAINTS)

53. (Saints.) Harewood (Yorks)   54. (Saints.) Harewood (Yorks)
55. (Saints.) Burton Agnes (Yorks)   56. (Relatives.) Ryther (Yorks)

WEEPERS

57. Aldermaston (Berks). Tomb of Sir George Forster, d. 1539

58. Fawsley (Northants). Tomb of Sir Richd Knightley, d. 1534

59. Windsor (Berks). Weepers from tomb of Sir George Manners
60. Fawsley (Northants). Weepers from tomb of Sir Richd Knightley

61. Ashover (Derby). Weepers from tomb of Thos Babyngton, d. 1518
62. Kinlet (Salop). Weepers from tomb of Sir John Blount, d. 1531

63. Ross (Heref). Tomb of Judge Rudhall, d. 1529
64. Barthomley (Cheshire). Angel   65. Stanford-on-Teme (Worc).
Weepers

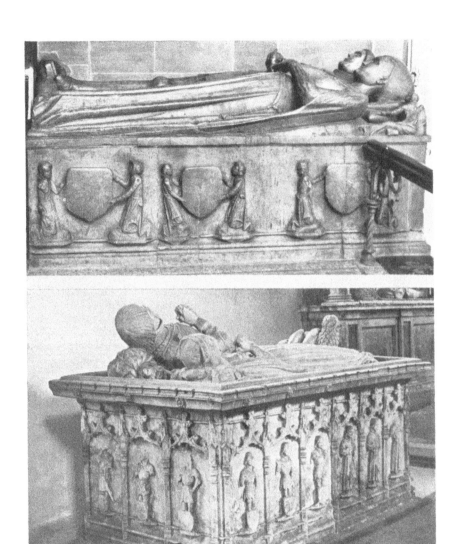

66. Macclesfield (Cheshire). Tomb of Sir John Savage, d. 1495
67. Thornhill (Yorks). Tomb of Sir John Savill, d. 1481

68. Clifton Campville (Staffs)
69. Ashover (Derby). Saints and weepers

71. Millom (Cumberland). Tomb of
Sir J. Hudleston, d. 1494. Angels

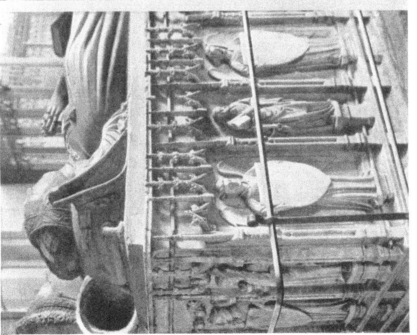

70. Tong (Salop). Tomb of Sir Richd Vernon,
d. 1451. Saints and angels

72. Tong (Salop). Angels
73. Dodford (Northants). Angels from tomb of Sir J. Cressy

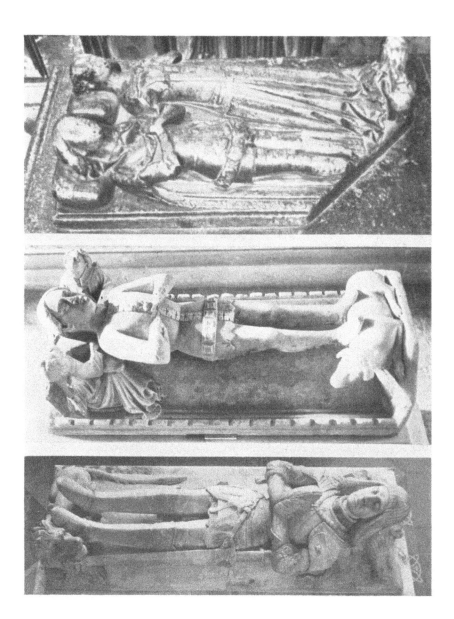

74. Small effigies. Westminster
75.   ,,   ,,   Haccombe (Devon)
76.   ,,   ,,   Youlgreave (Derby)

77. Ratcliffe-on-Soar (Notts). Ralph Sacheverell, d. 1539
78. Kedleston (Derby). A member of the Curzon family

79. Apethorpe (Northants). Small effigy with Coronation of the Virgin
as canopy

80. Abergavenny (Mon). End of Tomb

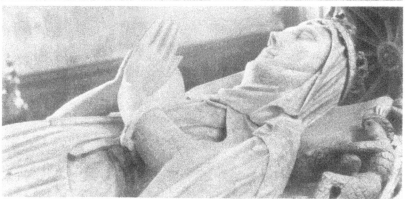

81. Wimborne (Dorset). Duke of Somerset, d. 1444
82. Ewelme (Oxon). Duchess of Suffolk, d. 1477
83. Callington (Cornwall). Lord Willoughby de Broke, d. 1503

INSIGNIA OF THE GARTER

84. Ashwellthorpe (Norf). Sir Edmund de Thorpe, d. 1417. SS

85. Ashwellthorpe (Norf). Lady Thorpe. SS

86. Longford (Derby). SS.

87. Holme Pierrepont (Notts). Y

HEADS AND COLLARS

88. Willoughby-in-the-Wolds (Notts).
       Salet
90. Methley (Yorks). SS

89. Weobley (Heref). SS

91. Bromsgrove (Worc). SS

HEADS AND COLLARS

92. Harewood (Yorks). SS
94. Harewood (Yorks). Y

93. Staindrop (Durham). SS
95. Harewood (Yorks). SS and roses

HEADS AND COLLARS

96. Swine (Yorks). Camail   97. Puddletown (Dorset). Salet
98. Norbury (Derby). Y   99. Merevale (Warw). Salet

HEADS AND COLLARS

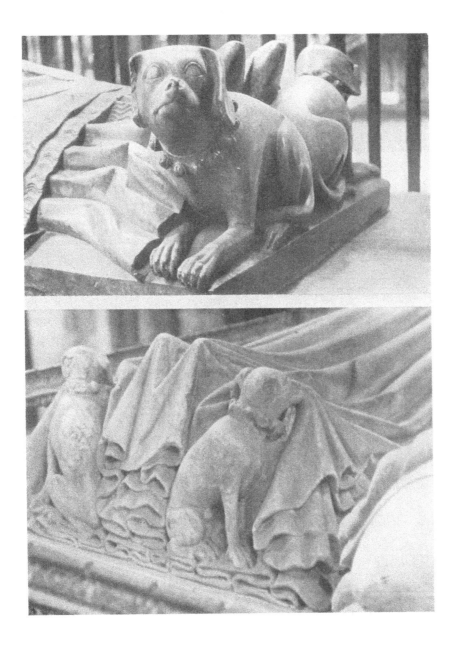

100. Westminster. Abp Langham. Dogs
101. Arundel (Sussex). Countess of Arundel. Dogs

102. Layer Marney (Essex). Sir Wm Marney, d. 1360. Lion
103. Wells (Som). Bp Harewell. Hares

104. Staindrop (Durham). Earl of Westmorland. Clerks
105. Lowick (Northants). Earl of Wiltshire. Bedesmen
106. Norbury (Derby). Sir R. Fitzherbert. Bedesman

107. Harewood (Yorks). Sir R. Redman. Bedesman

108. Wingfield (Suff). Duke of Suffolk. Crest

109. Swine (Yorks). Pointed sabatons

110. Ratcliffe-on-Soar (Notts). Square-toed sabatons

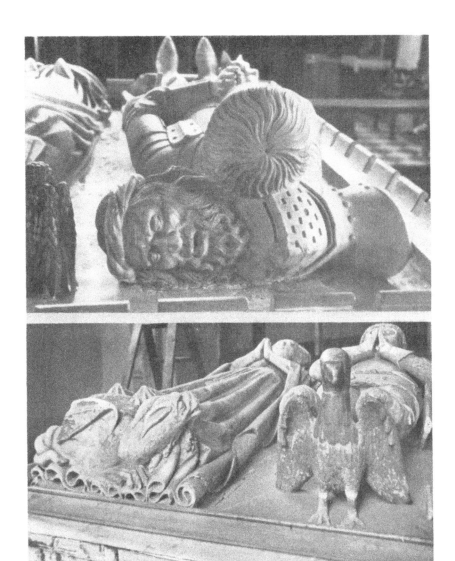

111. Lingfield (Surrey). Lord Cobham. Crest
112. Dennington (Suff). Lord Bardolf. Hawk and wyvern

113. Berkeley (Glouc). Nebuly

114. Harewood (Yorks). Widow's barbe and veil

115. South Cowton (Yorks). Truncated flapped

116. Lingfield (Surrey). Widow's barbe and veil

LADIES' HEAD-DRESSES

117. Hanbury (Staffs). Sir John de Hanbury, *c.* 1300
118. Gloucester. Edward II, d. 1327
119. Westminster. Prince John of Eltham, d. 1337
120. York. Prince William of Hatfield, d. 1346
121. Tewkesbury (Glouc). Sir Hugh Despenser, d. 1349

EFFIGIES, PERIOD I

122. Gloucester. Edward II
123. Tewkesbury (Glouc). Sir Hugh Despenser, d. 1349

124. Durham. Bp Hatfield, d. 1381
125. Winchester. Bp Edington, d. 1366
126. Wells. Bp Harewell, d. 1386
127. Gloucester. Abbot Seabroke, d. 1457
128. Sawley (Derby). Prebendary Bothe, d. 1496

ECCLESIASTICS

129. Wantage (Berks). Sir Wm Fitzwarren, d. 1361
130. Ashton (Northants). Johan de Herteshull, d. 1365
131. London, Gt St Helen's. John Oteswich, c. 1400
132. Hull. Sir Wm de la Pole, d. 1366

133. East Harling (Norf). Nebuly head-dress

134. East Harling (Norf). Bascinet and camail

135. Penmynydd (Anglesey). Ridged bascinet

136. Beaumaris (Anglesey). Salet

137. Greystoke (Cumberland). Baron of Greystoke
138. Arundel (Sussex). Earl of Arundel

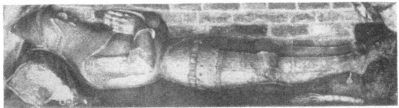

139. Bures (Suff) (from Colne Priory)
140. Clifton (Notts). Sir Gervase Clifton (?)
141. Clifton (Notts). Dame Alice Clifton, wife of above
142. Nuttall (Notts). Sir Robert Cokefield
143. Spratton (Northants). Sir John Swinford, d. 1371

EFFIGIES, PERIOD II

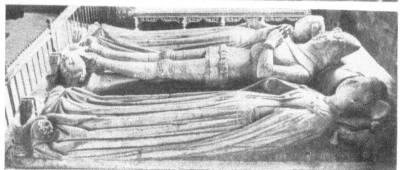

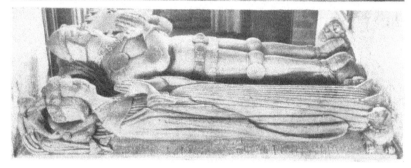

144. Effigies, Period II. Swine (Yorks)
145.   ,,   ,,   Swine (Yorks)
146.   ,,   ,,   Staindrop (Durham). Ralph Nevill, Earl of
                                Westmorland, d. 1425
147. Effigies, Period III. Harewood (Yorks)

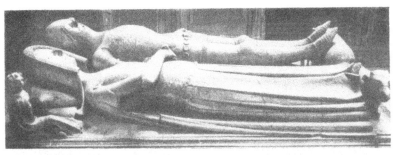

148. Effigies, Period II.   Warwick. Thos Beauchamp, Earl of Warwick,
        d. 1371
149.   ,,   ,,   Elford (Staffs). Sir John Arderne (?), d. 1408
150.   ,,   ,,   Strelley (Notts)
151. Effigies, Period III. Aston-on-Trent (Derby)

152. Haversham (Bucks). Lady Clinton, d. 1422
153. Northleigh (Oxon). Sir Wm Wilcote, d. 1411
154. West Tanfield (Yorks). Lady Marmion

155. Polesworth (Warw). Isabel Cockayne, d. 1447
156. Bunbury (Cheshire). Sir Hugh Calveley, d. 1393
157. Meriden (Warw). Sir John Wyard, d. 1404

158. Willoughby-in-the-Wolds (Notts). Sir Hugh Willoughby, d. 1448
159. Swine (Yorks). A member of the family of Hilton, c. 1410

160. Wells (Som). Priest
161. Westminster. Cardinal Abp Langham, d. 1376

162. Winchester. Bp William of Wykeham, d. 1404
163.   ,,   Bp William of Wykeham. Clerks at feet

164. Bures (Suff). An Earl of Oxford, *c.* 1420
165. Hornby (Yorks). Sir John Conyers, d. 1422

166. Willoughby-in-the-Wolds (Notts). Sir Richd Willoughby (Judge), d. 1362 (?)
167. Harewood (Yorks). Sir Wm Gascoigne, d. 1419 (Judge)

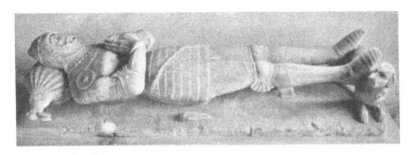

168. Wootton Wawen (Warw). John Harewell, d. 1428
169. Tideswell (Derby)
170. Merevale (Warw)
171. London, St Katharine's Chapel. Duke of Exeter, d. 1447

EFFIGIES, PERIOD III

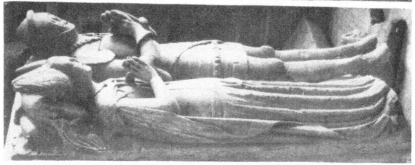

172. Porlock (Som)
173. East Shefford (Berks). Sir Thos Fettiplace
174. Ashbourne (Derby). Sir J. Cockayne, d. 1447
175. Bottesford (Leics). John, Lord Rous, d. 1421

EFFIGIES, PERIOD III

176. Dennington (Suff). Lord Bardolf, K.G., d. 1441
177. Stanton Harcourt (Oxon). Sir Robert Harcourt, K.G., d. 1471

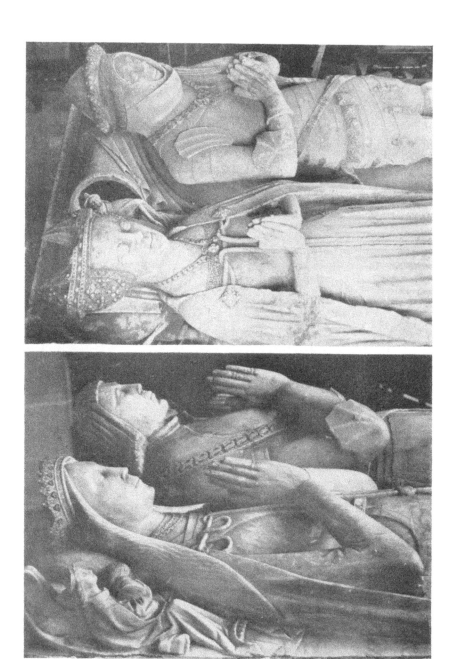

178. Dennington (Suff). Lord Bardolf, d. 1441
179. Elford (Staffs). Sir Wm Smythe, d. 1525

180. Lowick (Northants). Ralph Greene, d. 1419
181. Tong (Salop). Sir Richard Vernon, d. 1451

182. Canterbury. King Henry IV, d. 1413
183. Ewelme (Oxon). Duchess of Suffolk, d. 1477
184. Canterbury. Abp Stratford, d. 1348

85. Canterbury. Queen Joan, d. 1437

37. Over Peover (Cheshire). Lady Mainwaring

186. Methley (Yorks). Sir R. and Lady Waterton

188. Arundel (Sussex). Countess of Arundel

189. Burghill (Heref). Sir John Milbourne, *c.* 1450 (?)
190. Canterbury. Margaret Holland, d. 1437; Earl of Somerset, d. 1410;
Duke of Clarence, d. 1421

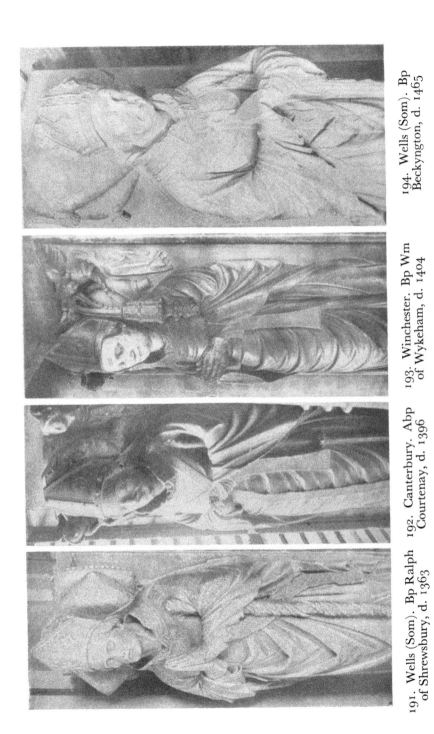

191. Wells (Som). Bp Ralph
of Shrewsbury, d. 1363

192. Canterbury. Abp
Courtenay, d. 1396

193. Winchester. Bp Wm
of Wykeham, d. 1404

194. Wells (Som). Bp
Beckyngton, d. 1465

ECCLESIASTICS

195. Nottingham. John Salmon (Mayor), d. 1416

196. Ryther (Yorks). Sir Wm Ryther, d. 1475

197. Exeter. Bp Stafford, d. 1419
198. Chichester. Bp Shirburne, d. 1536

199. Over Peover (Cheshire). Sir Randle Mainwaring, d. 1456
200. Cheadle (Cheshire). Sir J. Hondford, d. 1461; Sir J. Hondford, d. 1473

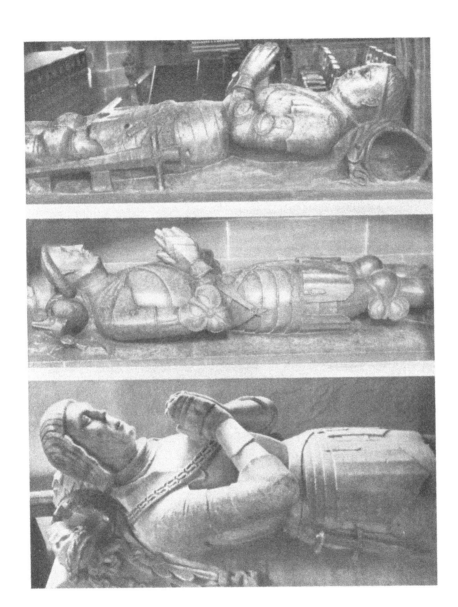

201. Macclesfield (Cheshire). Sir John Savage, d. 1463 (?)
202.   „   „   A member of the family of Downes of Shrigley
                                  c. 1470–80
203. Little Chart (Kent). Sir John Darell, d. 1509

204. Bottesford (Leics). Wm, Lord Rous, d. 1414
205. Lingfield (Surrey). Sir R. Cobham, d. 1446
206. Norbury (Derby). Sir Nicholas Fitzherbert, d. 1473

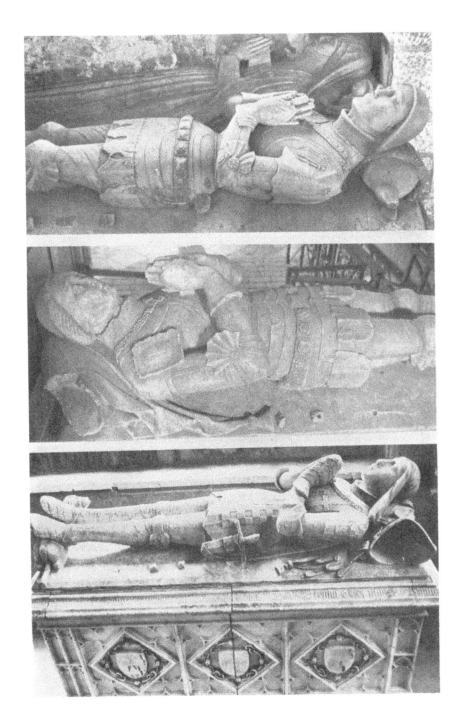

207. Harewood (Yorks)
208. Halsham (Yorks)
209. Lowick (Northants). Earl of Wiltshire, d. 1498

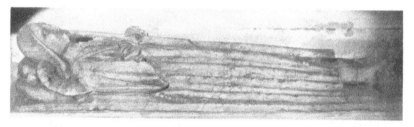

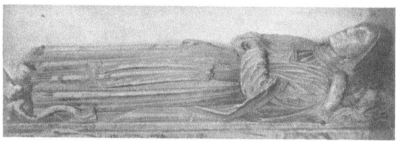

210. Ashby-de-la-Zouch (Leics). Pilgrim
211. Glastonbury (Som). A lay bursar
212. Dunmow Priory (Essex)
213. Norbury (Derby). Sir R. Fitzherbert, d. 1483
214. Puddletown (Dorset)

EFFIGIES, PERIOD IV

215. Dodford (Northants). Sir John Cressy, d. 1444

216. Ash (Kent)

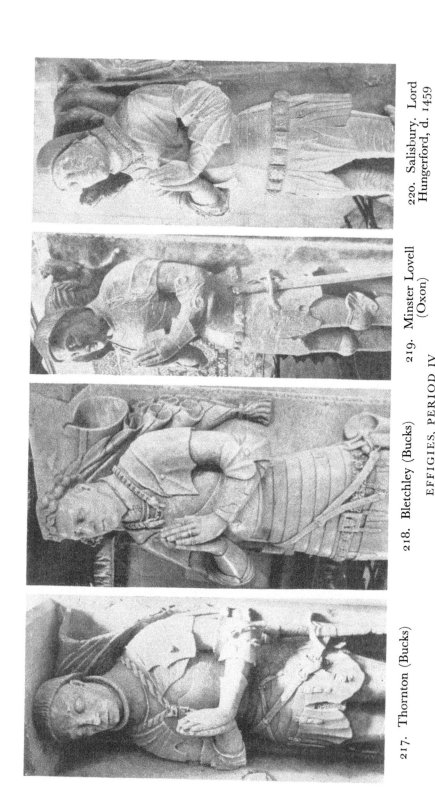

217. Thornton (Bucks)

218. Bletchley (Bucks)

219. Minster Lovell (Oxon)

220. Salisbury. Lord Hungerford, d. 1459

EFFIGIES, PERIOD IV

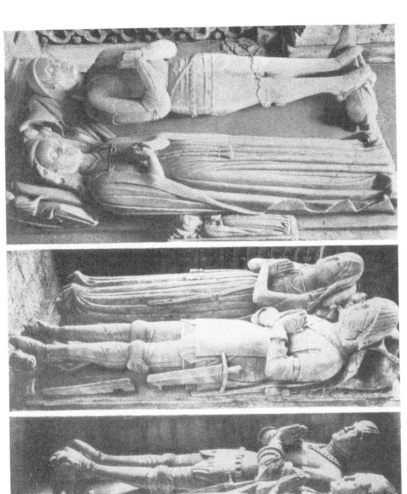

221. Burton Agnes (Yorks). Sir Walter Griffith, d. 1481
222. Harewood (Yorks). Sir J. Nevill, d. 1482
223. Methley (Yorks). Lord Welles, d. 1461
224. South Cowton (Yorks). Sir Richd Conyers, d. 1493

EFFIGIES, PERIOD IV

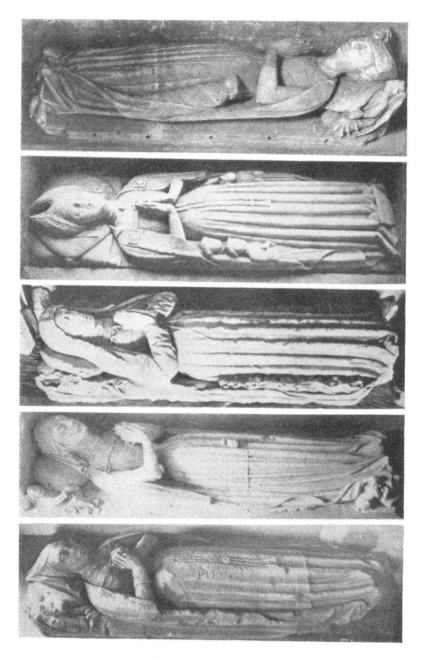

225. Kinlet (Salop)
226. Horwood (Devon)
227. Stourton Caundle (Dorset)
228. Thornton (Bucks)
229. Ilton (Som)

LADIES

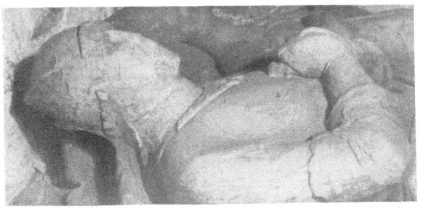

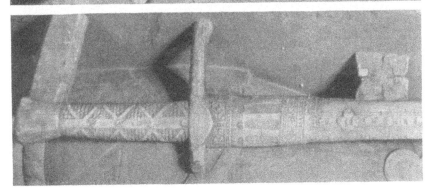

230. Kidderminster (Worc). Knight in Salet
231. Melbury Sampford (Dorset). Knight in Salet. Y
232. Meriden (Warw). Sir J. Wyard's sword-hilt

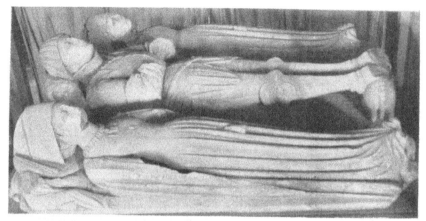

233. Marnhull (Dorset)
234. Thornhill (Yorks). Sir J. Savill, d. 1431
235. Ryther (Yorks). Sir Wm Ryther, d. 1475

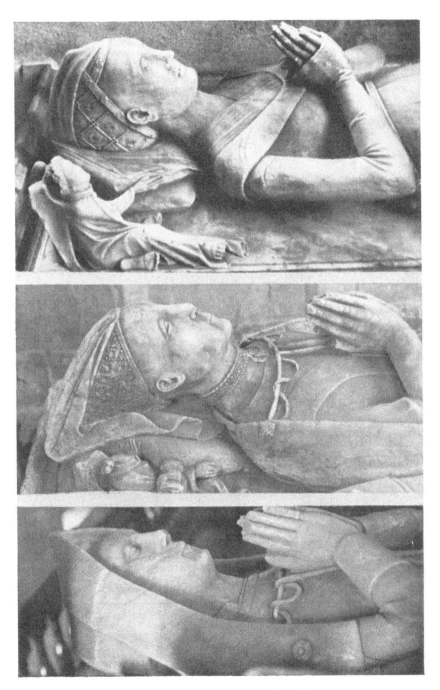

236. Clifton (Notts). Dame Alice Clifton
237. Norbury (Derby). Lady Fitzherbert
238. Godshill (Isle of Wight). Lady Leigh

239. Salisbury. Lord Hungerford, d. 1459

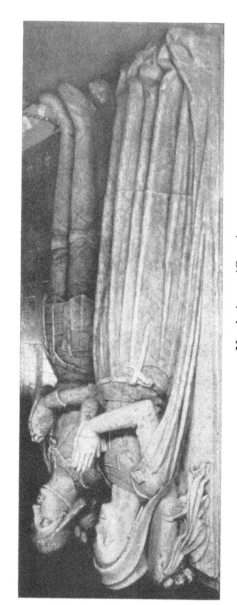

240. North Aston (Oxon)

241. Bakewell (Derby). Small tomb
242. London, Gt St Helen's. Sir John Crosby, d. 1474

243. Harewood (Yorks). Sir Richd Redman (?)

244. Clifton (Beds)
245.   ,,   ,,

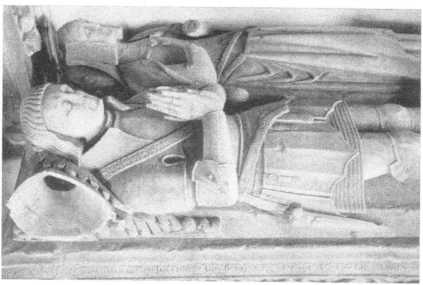

246. Holme Pierrepont (Notts). Sir Henry Pierrepont, d. 1499. Y
247. Ratcliffe-on-Soar (Notts). Ralph Sacheverell, d. 1539. SS

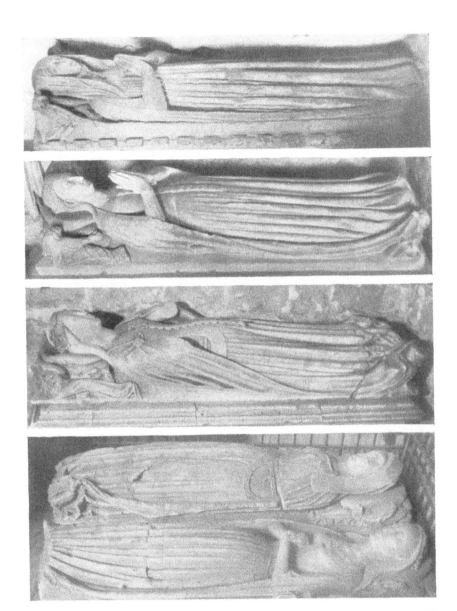

248. Leicester, Trinity Hospital. Mary de Bohun (?), d. 1394, 1st wife
of Henry IV
249. Burford (Salop). Princess Elizabeth (?), d. 1426, daughter of John
of Gaunt
250. Bromsgrove (Worc)
251. Astley (Warw). Lady L'Isle, d. 1483, and Marchioness of Dorset (?),
d. 1530

LADIES

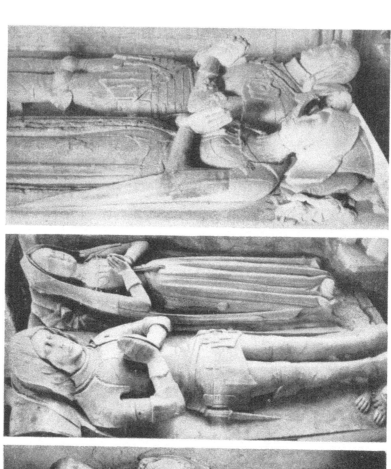

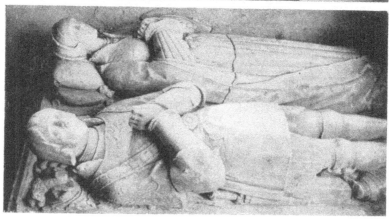

252. Kinlet (Salop). Sir Humphrey Blount, d. 1478
253. Chipping Norton (Oxon). Richard Croft, d. 1502
254. Eye (Heref). Sir George Cornwall (?), d. 1563

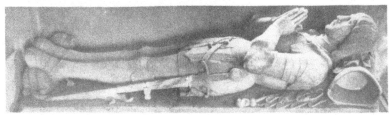

255. Eye (Heref). *c.* 1510–20
256. Elford (Staffs). Sir Wm Smythe, d. 1525
257. Holme Pierrepont (Notts). Sir H. Pierrepont, d. 1499
258. Radbourne (Derby). John Pole, *c.* 1500
259. Ashover (Derby). Thos. Babyngton, d. 1518

EFFIGIES, PERIOD V

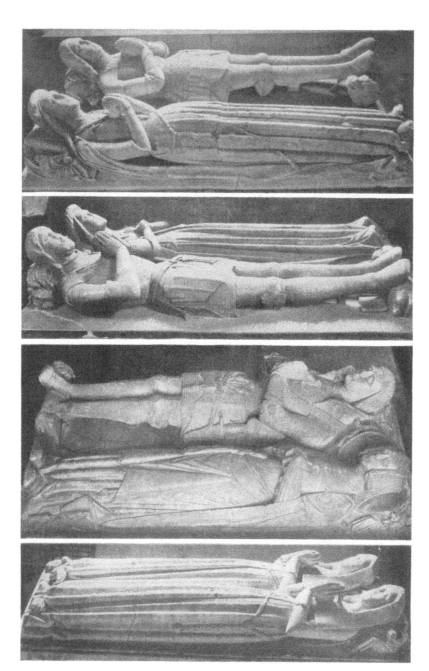

260. Thurlaston (Leics). John Turville, d. 1509
261. Batley (Yorks). Sir Wm Mirfield, d. 1496
262. Castle Donington (Leics). Robt Hazelrig, d. 1529
263. Prestwold (Leics)

EFFIGIES, PERIOD V

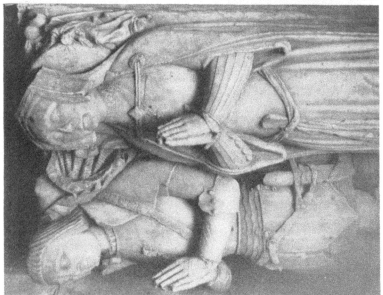

264. Middle Claydon (Bucks). 265. Duffield (Derby). Sir Roger Mynors, 266. Salisbury. Sir John
Lady Margaret Gyffard, d. 1536 Cheyney, K.G., d. 1509
d. 1539

267. Sheriff Hutton (Yorks). Edward Prince of Wales (?), d. 1484
268. Lockington (Leics). Lady Elizabeth Ferrers, c. 1500
269. Chilton (Suff). George Crane, d. 1491
270. Strelley (Notts). John Strelley, d. 1501

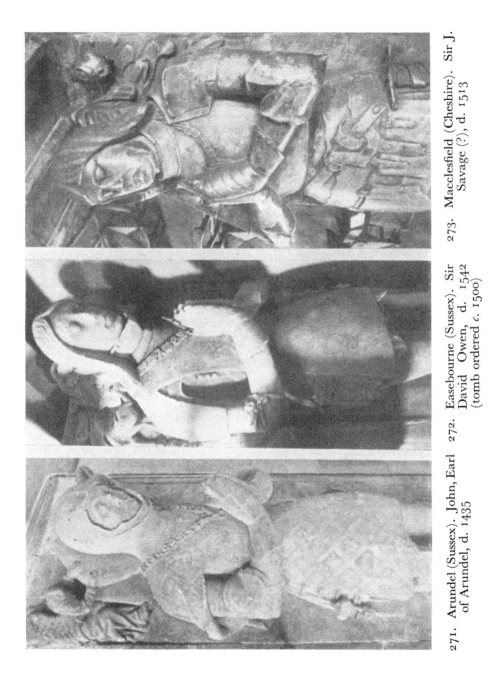

271. Arundel (Sussex). John, Earl   272. Easebourne (Sussex). Sir   273. Macclesfield (Cheshire). Sir J.
of Arundel, d. 1435   David Owen, d. 1542   Savage (?), d. 1513
                                                   (tomb ordered *c.* 1500)

274. Fawsley (Northants). Sir Richard Knightley, d. 1534

275. Wingfield (Suff). Duke of Suffolk, d. 1491
276. Aldermaston (Berks). Sir George Forster, d. 1539

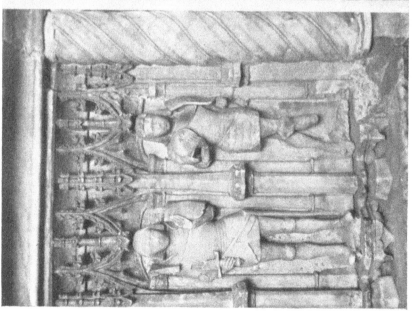

278. Aldermaston (Berks). Sir George Forster.
Head and helm

277. Aldermaston (Berks). Sir George Forster.
Weepers

279. Windsor (Berks). Sir George Manners, d. 1513

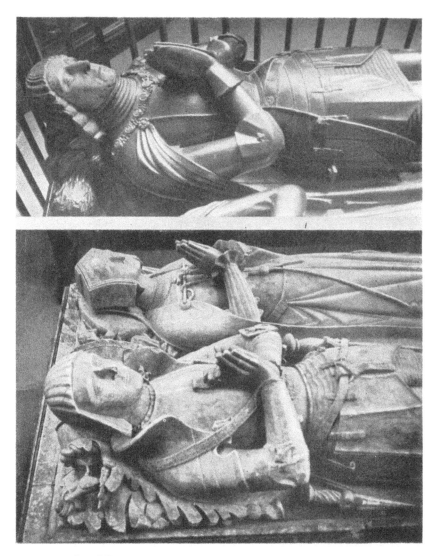

280. Westminster. Sir Giles Daubeny, K.G., d. 1506
281. Windsor (Berks). Sir George Manners, d. 1513

283. Wethersfield (Essex)

282. Chilton (Suff). Robert Crane,
d. 1500

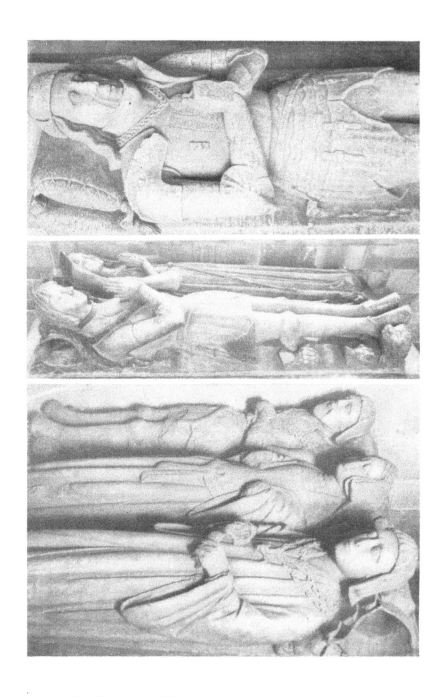

284. Bromham (Wilts). Lord St Amand, d. 1508
285. Coleshill (Warw). Sir Simon Digby, d. 1519
286. Coventry (Warw). Elizabeth Swillington, d. 1546

287. Barrow-on-Trent (Derby). Fourteenth-century priest
288. Yelvertoft (Northants). Fifteenth-century priest
289. Leicester. Bp Penny, d. 1520
290. Gloucester. Abbot Parker, d. 1535

ECCLESIASTICS

291. Bristol, St Mary Redcliffe. Wm Canynge (?), d. 1474

292. Yatton (Som). Sir Richd Newton (Judge), d. 1449; wife, d. 1475

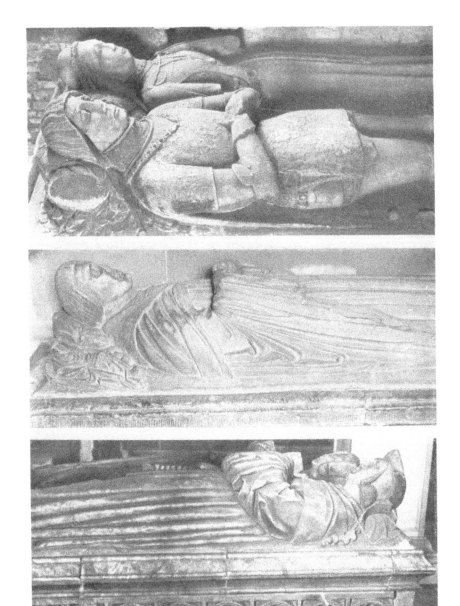

293. Upton (Northants). Sir Richard Knightley, d. 1537
294. Oxford, St Aldate's. John Noble, d. 1522
295. Ross (Heref). Judge Wm Rudhall, d. 1529

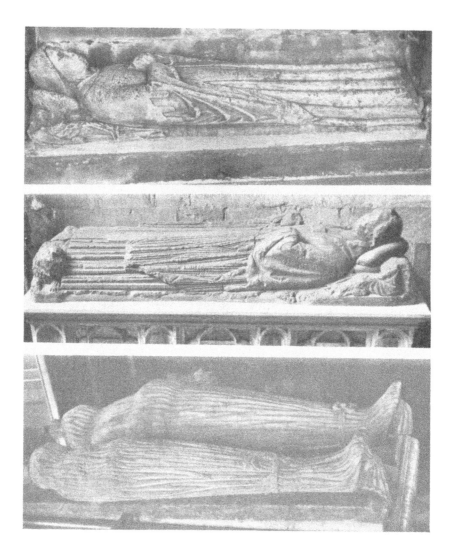

296. Halsall (Lancs). Priest
297. Hereford. Dean Harvey, d. 1500
298. Fenny Bentley (Derby). Shrouded effigies of the Beresford family

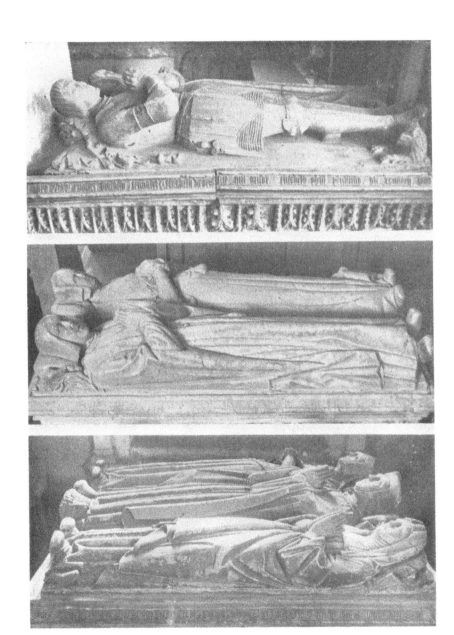

299. Llandaff (Wales). Sir Christopher Mathew, d. 1500
300. Newport (Salop)
301. Deene (Northants). Judge Sir Robt Brudenell, d. 1531

302. Ashby-de-la-Zouch (Leics). Earl of Huntingdon, d. 1561
303. Wroxeter (Salop). Lord Chief Justice Bromley, d. 1555

304. Stanford-on-Avon (Northants). Sir Thos Cave, d. 1558
305.   ,,   ,,   Sir Thos Cave. Weepers

INDEX TO TEXT

INDEX TO PLATES

CAMBRIDGE: PRINTED BY W. LEWIS, M.A., AT THE UNIVERSITY PRESS